THE HERITAGE OF INDIA SERIES (2)

A HISTORY OF KANARESE LITERATURE

THE HERITAGE OF INDIA SERIES (2)

A HISTORY OF KANARESE LITERATURE

BY

EDWARD P. RICE, B. A.

GYAN

Published by

Gyan Publishing House
5, Ansari Road
Daryaganj, New Delhi-110002
Phone: 011-47034999, 9811692060
E-mail: books@gyanbooks.com

Distribution Network
gyanbooks.com
India, USA, Canada, UK, Australia, France

ISBN: 978-81-212-8276-5 PB)
First Published, 1915

2nd Impression 2023

Printed at: Gyan Press, Delhi.

THE HERITAGE OF INDIA SERIES (2); A HISTORY OF KANARESE LITERATURE
Author: EDWARD P. RICE

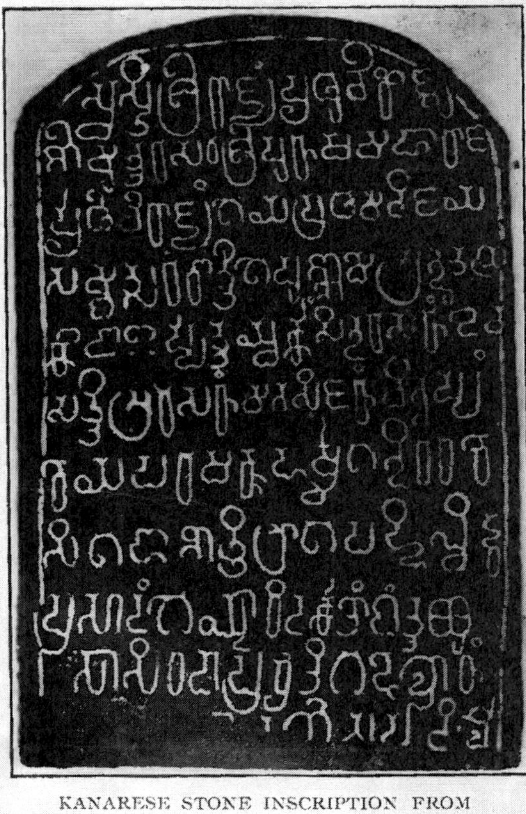

KANARESE STONE INSCRIPTION FROM TALKAD, A.D. 726.

Now in the Mysore University, Mysore.

THE HERITAGE OF INDIA SERIES

A HISTORY OF KANARESE LITERATURE

SECOND EDITION REVISED AND ENLARGED

BY

EDWARD P. RICE, B.A.

ASSOCIATION PRESS
5, RUSSELL STREET, CALCUTTA

LONDON: OXFORD UNIVERSITY PRESS
NEW YORK, TORONTO, MELBOURNE,
BOMBAY, CALCUTTA AND MADRAS
1921

DEDICATED

BY KIND PERMISSION

TO

PRĀKTANA VIMARŚA VICHAKSHAṆA,

RAO BAHĀDUR,

R. NARASIṀHĀCHĀRYA, M.A., M.R.A.S.,

DIRECTOR OF ARCHÆOLOGICAL RESEARCHES

IN MYSORE.

PREFACE TO THE FIRST EDITION

FIFTY years ago very few, even of the Kanarese people themselves, had any idea of the range of Kanarese literature, or of the relative age of the books which constitute it. Our present knowledge is the fruit of patient work on the part of a small number of painstaking scholars, who have laboriously pieced together the scattered information contained in inscriptions on stone and copper and in the colophons and text of palm-leaf manuscripts.

It is the practice of Kanarese poets to preface their works, not only with invocations of the gods and of the saints of old time, but also with the praise of former poets. This practice is of very great historical value, for it enables us to place the poets in their relative chronological order. As in many instances the writers received patronage from some reigning king, the mention of the name of the royal patron enables us further to give to many of the poets an approximately correct date. In this way a list of Kanarese poets can be drawn up in fairly correct order. The result shows that Kanarese has a literature of vast extent, reaching back till its beginnings are lost in the mists of time in the early centuries of the Christian era.

The first modern scholars to give with any fulness a connected view of Kanarese literature were the German missionaries, Würth and Kittel. The latter in 1875 prefixed a valuable essay on Kanarese Literature to his edition of Nāgavarma's *Prosody*. Since then a vast deal of additional information has been obtained, more especially through the researches of Mr. Lewis Rice, C.I.E., Director of Archæological Researches in Mysore, and his assistants and successor.

I am not aware that there is any separate volume in the English language giving a history of Kanarese literature. The most readable general account is to be found in Mr. Lewis Rice's *Gazetteer of Mysore*, Vol. I, and in his *Mysore and Coorg from the Inscriptions*. Fuller details are contained in his introduction to Bhaṭṭākalanka's *Karṇāṭaka Śabdānuśāsana*, a bulky volume now out of print; and in the *Karṇāṭaka Kavi Charite* or "Lives of the Kanarese Poets," by Messrs. R. and S. G. Narasiṁhāchārya, respectively Officer in charge of Archæological Researches and Kanarese Translator to the Government of Mysore. The last-named work being written in Kanarese is available only for those who know that language. Only Part I has so far been published, which carries the history up to the end of the fourteenth century. It gives illustrative extracts from the works described. The present popular account of Kanarese literature is based on the above-named authorities, to whom acknowledgement is hereby unreservedly made. Without their researches this work could not have been written.

The enumeration of a long series of little known writers cannot be other than tedious to the reader. I have endeavoured to mitigate this effect by introducing as much local colour as was available, and by sketching in as a background an outline of the times in which the poets lived and the atmosphere of religious faith and custom in which they moved. For the sake of English readers I have also explained many Indian terms which require no explanation for the Indian reader.

By desire of the Editors, renderings have been given of a few illustrative passages from typical works belonging to different periods. In these, for reasons partially indicated in Chapter X, the attempt has been rather to express the general spirit of the original than to offer a closely literal translation. Graces due to alliteration, rhythm, vocabulary, and double meaning are, of course, lost in any translation.

The systematic historical study of Kanarese literature is of such recent origin, and every year is adding so much to our knowledge, that on numerous points there will soon be available fuller and more accurate information than that presented in the present volume. My brother, Mr. Lewis Rice, has kindly read through the manuscript and made various suggestions.

Hassocks, E. P. R.
October, 1915.

PREFACE TO THE SECOND EDITION

THE call for a second edition made it desirable that the account here given of Kanarese literature should be brought, as far as possible in a book of this size, up to the present state of our information. This has been facilitated by the publication, in the meantime, of the second volume of Mr. Narasiṁhāchārya's *Lives of the Kanarese Poets*, bringing the record up to 1700 A.D. Much of the fresh information brought to light in that volume has been here embodied, and so made available for those who cannot read that book in the original Kanarese. Its dates also have generally been followed, as being based on the fullest and most recent data.

In other respects also this edition differs from the former. Some re-arrangement of matter has been made. The account of Liṅgāyat literature has been extended and largely rewritten. Much has been added to the accounts of Jaina and Vaishṇava literature also. An attempt has been made to elucidate more fully one or two obscure points, such as the difference between the Jaina and Brāhmanical versions of the Rāmāyaṇa, the meaning of Syādvāda, the origin of the Liṅgāyat Revival, etc. To make room for this additional matter, the Appendices have been omitted; and also the account of the Kingdoms and Dynasties of the Kanarese country. As much as seemed necessary on these subjects has been inserted elsewhere in the book. The writer has gladly availed himself of the opportunity to correct minor inaccuracies, some of which were due to the haste, and some to the war conditions, under which the first edition was produced. If, in its new form, this little compilation prove more useful and reliable to students of Kanarese literature; and if, by disclosing the contents of that literature to others, it contributes toward a better understanding and greater mutual sympathy between East and West, it will have fulfilled the writer's earnest desire.

Hassocks, E. P. R.
July, 1920.

CONTENTS

I

THE KANARESE LANGUAGE AND COUNTRY

The Dravidian Languages. Kanarese is one of the Dravidian languages, which are the vernaculars of South India, and which are wholly unrelated to the Aryan languages spoken in North India. The other literary members of the family are Tamil, Telugu and Malayalam. A line drawn from Goa, on the West Coast, to Rājmahal, on the Ganges, will approximately divide the Dravidian languages on the south from the Aryan languages on the north. There is a large population of Dravidian *race* north of this; but they no longer speak a Dravidian language. No close connection has been shown between the Dravidian languages and any other languages of the world, if we except Brahūi, a non-literary language of Belūchistān. Certain words and forms seem to point to a connection with the ancient Median language used on the Behistun monument (and perhaps with Akkadian). Affinities are also said to exist with the Finnish of North Europe and the Ostiak of Siberia. These call for fuller investigation.[1] The Dravidians seem to have occupied their present seats from extreme antiquity. One of the earliest traces of this group of languages is found in the fact that the peacocks imported into Jerusalem by King Solomon 1000 B.C., and which must have come from the west coast of India, have a Tamil name.[2]

[1] See Caldwell's *Comparative Grammar of the Dravidian Languages*.

[2] Hebrew *tukki* = Tamil *tokai*, which, in ancient Tamil, meant "peacock."

The Kanarese Country. The population speaking Kanarese is about ten millions. The extent of country in which it is now the vernacular is shown in the map at the end of this volume. It includes the whole of Mysore, the western half of the Nizam's Dominions and the southern (so-called "South Mahratta and North Canara") districts of the Bombay Presidency, together with the districts of South Canara and Bellary in the Madras Presidency. With the exception of the Western Ghats and the strip of land at their feet, the whole of this tract is an upland plain from 1,200 to 3,000 feet above the sea, with a flat or gently undulating surface, draining off to the East.

In the *Kavirājamārga* (A.D. 850) the Kanarese country is described as extending from the Kāveri to the Godāvari; which shows that the linguistic area at that time extended further north than at present. Inscriptions, manuscripts, local names and other evidence prove that Kolhapur, where the chief language now is Marāṭhī, was once in the Kanarese area. Also in Sholapur town and district there are many Kanarese inscriptions. The northern limits of Kanarese were probably pushed back by the Marāṭhā raids and conquests.

The Name of the Language. Kanarese is called by its own sons *Kannaḍa* or *Karṇāṭaka*. The English name is a corrupt form derived from the early Portuguese, who entered the country through what is now known as North Canara, and spoke of the country and people as *Canarijs*. When the English settled on the East Coast, all South India, from the river Kṛishṇa to Cape Comorin, was under the rule of a Kanarese dynasty, reigning at Vijayanagar, and was known as the Karṇāṭaka Realm. Hence the name "Carnatic" has come to be popularly applied to the coastal plains south of Madras, although these are Tamil-speaking districts and quite outside the Kanarese country proper.

Earliest Specimens. In a Greek papyrus of the second century found at Oxyrrhynchus, in Egypt, occur a few words quoted from some Indian language, which Dr. Hultzsch thinks can be identified with Kanarese (See

J.R.A.S., 1904, p. 399). If this be so, this will be the earliest extant trace of Kanarese. Among the earliest inscriptions, of approximately known date, written in the Kanarese language, are the following, the text and translation of which can be seen in the *Epigraphia Carnātica* (quoted as E.C.). Those marked with an asterisk are there given also in facsimile.

	Date
Rock inscriptions at Śravaṇa Beḷgoḷa ; E.C. II, 1-21, 23, 26-35. No. 26* is quoted and translated below (p. 22).	Early
On a stone in temple at Siragunda ; E.C. VI, Chikmagalūr 50.*	c. 500
On a stone in temple at Kigga ; E.C. VI, Koppa 37.	c. 675
On a stone found at Talkād, now in Victoria Jubilee Institute, Mysore ; E.C. III, Tirumakūdlu Narsipura 11.* It is figured as frontispiece to this book.	726
On a vīrakal found at Doḍḍahunḍi representing the death of the Ganga king, Nītimārga ; E.C. III, TN 91.* It is now in the Bangalore Museum.	c. 869
On a sculptured stone from a temple, in Bēgūr, but now in the Bangalore Museum ; E.C. IX, Bangalore 83.*	c. 890
On a stone at Bellatūr, a lengthy inscription by the poet, Malla, recording the suicide by fire of a Śūdra woman whose husband had been put to death for killing a kinsman, apparently in a wrestling match ; E.C. IV, Heggaḍadēvankōṭe 18.	1057

The Kanarese Alphabet and Written Character. It is to Sanskrit scholars from the north that Kanarese is indebted for its reduction to writing and its introduction into the world of literature. The grammatical terms and arrangement follow Sanskrit models.

The *Alphabet* is consequently syllabic, and follows the orderly arrangement of the Sanskrit alphabet. It even includes forms for ten aspirates, two sibilants and certain vowels and a semi-vowel not required for Dravidian words ; but there have been added five characters (ĕ, ŏ, ḷa, ṟa, ḻa,) for sounds not occurring in Sanskrit. The universal practice of making children recite the *Amara Kośa* (a metrical Sanskrit glossary) from the very beginning of their education has helped to Sanskritise the pronunciation of the language. The aspirates are now freely used in indigenous words ; and of its own characteristic letters two have dropped out of use—*ḻa* about the twelfth century, and *ṟa* about the eighteenth century.[1]

"The written character which is common to Kannaḍa and Telugu, and which spread over the south and was carried even to Java, is derived, through that of the cave inscriptions in the west of India, from the South Asoka character, or that of all his inscriptions except in the extreme north-west of the Panjab. It belongs to about 250 B.C., prior to which date no specimens of writing have been discovered in India, though there are numerous earlier allusions to writing. This ancient alphabet has lately been satisfactorily proved by Dr. Bühler to be of Semitic origin. It is properly called the *Brahmi lipi*, and was introduced into India probably about 800 B.C." (*Mysore Gazetteer*, I, 491). For the study of the character in successive centuries the student is referred to Burnell's *South India Palæography* (Trübner, 1878), and to Bühler's *Indian Palæography*, a translation of which appeared in the *Indian Antiquary* for 1904.

Historic Changes. Dr. Kittel notes three stages in the history of the language during the past thousand years—*viz.* Ancient, Mediæval, and Modern.

The commencement of the second and third stages coincides approximately with the beginning of the Liṅgāyat and Vaishṇava literatures respectively. (See below, pp. 59 and 78; also Preface to Kittel's *Kannaḍa-English Dictionary*.)

It should be noted that the term "Ancient Kanarese" does not always denote an obsolete form of the language. For colloquial purposes it is, of course, obsolete; but its vocabulary and inflexions are still used for the purposes of poetry. The term, therefore, sometimes denotes a particular antique style of writing.

The Influence of Neighbouring Languages. As regards vocabulary, Kanarese is dependent on Sanskrit for practically all abstract, religious, scientific, and philo-

[1] Both these letters are still retained in Tamil, Malayālam and Baḍaga; and the *ṟa* is retained in Telugu also. See Kittel's *Kannaḍa Grammar*, p. 15 note.

sophical terms. Even the oldest extant Kanarese works abound in Sanskrit terms. Āṇḍayya (c. 1235) by a *tour de force* succeeded in excluding *tatsamas* (unchanged Sanskrit words) from his *Kabbigara Kāva* (see p. 44); but even he uses *tadbhavas* (naturalised Sanskrit words) which occur also freely in all inscriptions. It has been well said that Sanskrit, though not the mother of Kanarese, is entitled to be called its *foster-mother*, because it was owing to the vigour infused into it by Sanskrit that it was enabled to become a literary language. (*Essays on Kanarese Grammar, Comparative and Historical*, by R. Raghunātha Rau, B.A., Bangalore, 1894.)

Telugu seems to have had some influence in modifying Kanarese inflections. This was probably due to the extensive intercourse which always existed between the two language areas, which are not separated by any geographical barrier. Moreover, the two languages have a common alphabet; and their territories have sometimes been under a common or allied sovereignty. The Marāṭhī language has influenced the dialects of the north-west part of the country.

That the influence of Tamil has been only slight is partly due to the fact that the two peoples used very dissimilar alphabets. Moreover, the Eastern Ghats formed a geographical boundary between them, Tamil being mostly confined to the plains below, and Kanarese to the plateau above. But some modifications due to Tamil were probably introduced when Śrī-Vaishṇavism was adopted from Tamil teachers.

PERIODS OF THE HISTORY OF KANARESE LITERATURE

The history of Kanarese literature can best be divided into periods corresponding to the religious systems dominant in successive times.

1. Until the middle of the twelfth century it is exclusively *Jaina*, and Jaina literature continues to be prominent for long after. It includes all the more ancient, and many of the most eminent, of Kanarese writings.

2. *Liṅgāyat* literature commences from about A.D. 1160, when Basavāchārya revived the ancient Vīraśaiva, or Liṅgāyat religion—an evolution which was signalised by a great outburst of Vīraśaiva literary activity, wholly different from that of the Jainas.

3. The *Vaishṇava* revival, beginning under Rāmānujāchārya in the beginning of the twelfth century, continued by Madhvāchārya (about 1250) and reinforced by Chaitanya (1500), introduced a period in which *Brāhmanic* thought became dominant, an ascendance which has continued up till the present time. Its marked effect upon Kanarese literature may be said to commence from the date of the Kanarese version of the Bhārata (c. 1440).

4. A *Modern* period is now in its early stages, which has been brought into being by the impact of Western thought and the influence of English literature.

The whole course of the history may be compared to a river receiving tributaries. During the first millennium of its course it is an unmingled stream of Jaina thought. In the twelfth century this is joined by the stream of Vīraśaivism ; and the two streams, like the Rhone and Saone at Lyons, flow side by side without mingling. In the beginning of the sixteenth century these two are joined by a Vaishṇava affluent ; and the united stream flows on until in the nineteenth century it is broadened and much modified by a great inrush of Western thought.

These different sections of Kanarese literature differ not only in religious background, but also in literary form. Jaina works are generally in *champu*, *i.e.* mingled prose and verse, the verse being in a great variety of metres and evincing great literary skill. Much Liṅgāyat literature is in prose ; its poetry is mostly in six-lined stanzas, called *shaṭpadi* ; some is in three-lined *tripadi* or in *ragaḷe*. The longer Brāhmanical works are also in *shaṭpadi* ; but there are beside many lyrical compositions to popular airs. The literature of the Modern period is mostly in prose ; but a popular form of composition is *yakshagāna*.

II

THE JAINA PERIOD

TO A.D. 1160

Śrīmat parama gambhīra syādvād-āmogha-lāñchanam
Jīyāt trailokya-nāthasya śāsanam Jina śāsanam.

"May the sacred Jaina doctrine, the doctrine of the lord of the three worlds, be victorious;—the supreme, profound *syādvāda*, the token of unfailing success." This couplet is placed at the head of most Jaina inscriptions.

THE JAINA RELIGION IN THE KANARESE COUNTRY

Up to the middle of the twelfth century practically every Kanarese writer belonged to the Jaina faith; and even after that date for several centuries some of the most scholarly writers continued to be Jainas. It is, therefore, well to preface the record of this period of the literature with a few notes on the Jaina religion and its connection with the Kanarese country. This is, indeed, necessary in order that there may be a suitable background for the story.

Its Dominance in the Kanarese Country. For more than a thousand years after the beginning of the Christian era, Jainism was the religion professed by most of the rulers of the Kanarese people. The Ganga kings of Talkāḍ, the Rāshṭrakūṭa and Kalachurya kings of Mānyakhēṭa, and the early Hoysalas were all Jainas. Although the Kadambas and early Chalukyas were of the Brāhmanical faith, they were very tolerant of Jainism, and did not withhold patronage from its writers. Hiuen Tsang, in the seventh century, records that he found the Jainas very numerous in these parts; and they seem to have been very successful in disputation with their rivals, the Buddhists. The Pāṇḍyan kings of Madura were Jainas; and Jainism was dominant in Gujarāt and Kāthiāwār. On the other hand, the Pallavas of Kāñchī, and the Cholas of Uraiyūr and Tanjore, were strongly Hindu and hostile to Jainism.

Its Introduction into South India. Jainism was introduced into South India at some period prior to the Christian era. An eminent Jaina leader, of the name of Bhadrabāhu, either in Pāṭaliputra or Ujjayini, anticipating a prolonged famine in North India, led a large community of Jainas towards the south, and travelled as far as the two rocky hills, now called Śravaṇa Beḷgoḷa ("Beḷgoḷa of the Jainas"), in the centre of the Mysore country. This is spoken of by the Jainas as the great Digambara migration, and marks an epoch in their history.

So far all scholars are agreed. Jaina traditions state that this Bhadrabāhu was the well-known *śruta kēvalin* (*i.e.* one of the six teachers who had complete knowledge of the Jaina Scriptures), who was a contemporary of Chandragupta, the founder of the Mauryan Empire. They say, further, that Chandragupta, who ceased to reign in 297 B.C. at the age of fifty, but of whose death the secular histories say nothing, laid aside his sovereignty to become a Jaina ascetic, and that he accompained Bhadrabāhu to the south, and was the sole attendant permitted to remain with him when, feeling that his end was approaching, he ascended the smaller hill at Śravaṇa Beḷgoḷa and took the vow of *sallēkhana*, or renunciation of life by voluntary starvation. Also that Chandragupta remained on the spot, and died there twelve years later by the same rite. Some scholars, on the other hand, are of opinion that the Bhadrabāhu in question lived in the first century before Christ, and that the Digambara migration to the south took place then.

Whatever may be the actual historical facts, the tradition about Chandragupta has for thirteen hundred years or more been accepted as true by the Jainas. Śravaṇa Beḷgoḷa became a place of pilgrimage. Many devotees, both male and female, including some of royal rank, took the vow of euthanasia on the same hill; and their piety and endurance are recorded in numerous inscriptions on the rocky hillside. The hill became gradually covered with temples, the most ancient being one named after Chandragupta. In A.D. 983 a unique monument was dedicated on the adjoining hill. A colossal image, 57½ feet high, of a nude Jaina ascetic, was carved out of the living rock on the summit of the hill. With serene and placid features it has stood there for almost a thousand years looking over the plain, whence it is visible for many miles.[1]

Principal Tenets. The Jaina religion is an offspring of the same movement of thought as that which produced Buddhism; and the two religions have many points of similarity. In neither is any cognisance taken of a Supreme Being, Creator and Ruler of the World. The reverence of the worshipper is bestowed upon certain men, who are regarded as having by ascetic practices gained complete mastery over bodily passions. These men are called *Jinas*, or victors, and *Tīrthaṅkaras* (or Tīrthakaras), that is, those who have crossed the ocean of human distraction and reached the shore of eternal placidity.[2] Twenty-four of these are especially named, the latest being Vardhamāna Mahāvīra, a slightly older contemporary of Gautama Buddha. The

[1] There are two similar images of the same saint, Gommaṭa, in the Tuluva country—one at Kārkaḷa, 41 feet high, dating from 1432; the other at Yēnūr, 35 feet, executed 1604. They are all on hill tops, and within the Kanarese country; and are said to be the largest free-standing statues in Asia (Vincent Smith's *History of Fine Art in India*). The name Gommaṭa does not occur elsewhere in India, and seems not to be known to the Jainas of the North. He is identified in Jaina works with Bāhubali, son of the first Tīrthankara, and brother of the Emperor Bharata.

[2] This was the original meaning. But modern Jainas use it in the sense of the Founder of the four *tīrthas* or orders (monks, nuns, lay-brothers and lay-sisters) that collectively constitute a Jaina Sangha (Stevenson, *Heart of Jainism*, p. xv).

images of these Tīrthankaras are set up in the temples, and reverenced as embodying the Jaina ideal of the conquering life. The legendary accounts of their lives, showing the greatness of their renunciation, and through what struggles they succeeded in snapping the bonds of *karma* and attaining complete detachment from the senses, form the subject of the Jaina *Purāṇas.* In choosing these as subjects for their poems they were actuated by the same motives as Milton when he wrote the *Paradise Lost*, or Cædmon when he sang of the *Creation.*

The following are the names of the Tīrthankaras, who all bear the epithet of *Nātha,* "Lord":

1. Ṛishabha	9. Pushpadanta	17. Kunthu
2. Ajita	10. Sītaḷa	18. Ara
3. Sambhava	11. Srēyāṁsa	19. Malli
4. Abhinandana	12. Vāsupūjya	20. Munisuvrata
5. Sumati	13. Vimala	21. Nami
6. Padmaprabha	14. Ananta	22. Nēmi
7. Supārśva	15. Ḍharma	23. Pārśva
8. Chandraprabha	16. Śānti	24. Vardhamāna

The lives of the last two closely resemble that of Gautama Buddha; for, like him, after attaining enlightenment, they travelled for many years over the plain of the Ganges, preaching and making disciples, till they died at an advanced age. They may be regarded as historical. The others are purely legendary. All of them are represented as having been Kshatriya princes of North India. All but two belonged to the Ikshvāku line of kings, and ruled over one or another of the states along the Ganges Valley. All but four passed to nirvāṇa from the Pārśvanātha Hill in Bengal. The first, Ṛishabha, is said to have been the father of Bāhubali (Gommaṭa) and of Bharata, the Emperor from whom India derives its name of Bhārata. The sixteenth, Śāntinātha, King of Hastinapura, is said to have been emperor of all India. From his time the Jaina religion, which had been intermittent before, became permanently established. The twentieth, Munisuvrata, and twenty-second, Neminātha, were of the Hari line, *i.e.* of the same family as Kṛishṇa. Hence their story is often called a Harivamśa. Like Kṛishṇa, they are represented as dark-hued. Neminātha was cousin to Kṛishṇa and Balarāma; and his nirvāṇa was from Girnār Hill in Kāthiāwār.

It will thus be seen that the Jaina ideal was asceticism. Many of the Jaina writers whose names appear in this book are spoken of as *munis* or *yatis*, *i.e.* men who practised the austerities of the ascetic life. The complete conquest of the weakness of the flesh expressed itself in the renunciation of clothing. The images in the Jaina temples of South India are all nude.[1] The Jainas are divided into two sects, *Digambaras* ("space-clad"), who, on occasion and as far as possible dispense with clothing altogether (as their founder, Mahāvīra, did); and *Śvētāmbaras* ("clad in white"). The yatis of the Kanarese country are Digambaras; but they wear a yellow robe, which they cast off when taking meals.

One of the most outstanding characteristics of the Jainas is the stress they lay on the duty of not taking animal life in any form. This is carried to such an extreme that Jaina monks wear a muslin cloth over their mouth, lest they should inadvertently breathe in a gnat; and they carry a small brush with which to sweep the path in front of them, lest they tread on a creeping insect. This scruple largely debars Jainas from engaging in agriculture.

The Vow of Sallekhana (called in Gujarāti, *Santhāro*). The most striking illustration of the self-repressive character of Jainism is the vow of *sallēkhana* referred to above. When old age, incurable disease, sore bereavement, disappointment, or any other cause, had taken away the joy of living, many resolute Jainas, like some Stoics of the West, would hasten Yama's tardy footsteps by taking the vow of euthanasia. In spite of the fact that the taking of life is the greatest sin conceivable to a Jaina, an exception was made in favour of the vow of voluntary starvation, which was looked upon as the highest proof of that victory over the bodily passions which made a perfect Jaina. From the earliest Christian centuries until the nineteenth century the practice has survived. Jainas still take the vow in their homes when death is imminent.

[1] In Gujarāt also, Digambara images are nude; but Śvetāmbara images are given loin-cloths (Mrs. Stevenson, *Heart of Jainism*, p. 250).

The most notable scene of the rite is at Śravaṇa Beḷgoḷa. The devotee would renounce all possessions and all earthly ties, and resort to the bare rocky hill at Śravaṇa Beḷgoḷa, immediately to the north of that on which the colossal statue to Gommaṭa stands. There keeping his mind free, on the one hand from relentings and on the other hand from impatience for death, and letting his thoughts dwell on those who had conquered the flesh before and had attained the state of the gods, he would simply await release by death. The rock is covered with inscriptions recording the steadfastness of those who have fulfilled the vow. Among them occur the names of royal personages. Indrarāja, the last of the Rāshṭrakūṭas of Mānyakhēṭa, being overwhelmed by the Western Chālukyas in A.D. 973, died by this vow at Śravaṇa Beḷgoḷa in 982. When Vishṇuvardhana's queen, Śāntala Dēvī, died, childless, at the very same time as her father also died, the widowed mother, Machikabbe, was disconsolate; and the more so that her son-in-law had abandoned the Jaina faith for Vaishṇavism. So she took the vow, and after severe fasting for one month, passed away. Of the numerous inscriptions upon the rock, some consist only of a single line. Others are more or less lengthy and florid. The first to be deciphered may be rendered as follows:

Swift fading as the rainbow's hue
Or lightning flash or morning dew,
To whom do pleasure wealth and fame
For many years remain the same?
Then why should I, whose thoughts aspire
To reach the highest good, desire
Here on the earth long days to spend?

Reflecting thus within his mind,
  The noble Nandi Sēn
All ties that bound to life resigned,
  To quit this world of pain.
And so this best of anchorites
  The World of Gods did gain.

Syádváda. Jainas always speak of their philosophical system under the name of *Syādvāda*. Their disputants glory in the conquering power of this doctrine, and their inscriptions are invariably prefaced with the śloka given at the head of this chapter, and in which the doctrine is extolled. *Syād* is the Sanskrit for "it may perhaps be," and *Syādvāda* may be rendered, "the affirmation of alternative possibilities," but it is a highly technical term.

The most helpful exposition of the meaning and importance of Syādvāda has been given by Prof. Jacobi.[1] He points out that it is best understood by considering its relation to the doctrines it was employed to oppose. The great contention of Advaitins was that there is only one really existing entity, the Ātman, the One-only-without-a-second (*ekādvitīyam*), and that this is permanent (*nitya*), all else being non-existent (*a-sat*), a mere illusion. Hence it was called the *ātma-vāda*, *eka-vāda* and *nitya-vāda*. Their stock argument was that just as there are no such entities as cup, jar, etc., these being only *clay* under various names and shapes—so all the phenomena of the universe are only various manifestations of the sole entity, *ātman*. The Buddhists, on the other hand, said that man had no real knowledge of any such permanent entity ; it was pure speculation, man's knowledge being confined to changing phenomena—growth, decay, death. Their doctrine was therefore called *anitya-vāda*. As against both these, the Jainas opposed a theory of *varying possibilities* of Being, or various points of view (*anekānta-vāda*). Clay, as a substance may be permanent ; but as a jar, it is impermanent—may come into existence, and perish. In other words, Being is not simple, as Advaitins assert, but complex ; and any statement about it is only *part* of the truth. The various possibilities were classed under seven heads (*sapta-bhanga*), each beginning with the word *syād*, which is combined with one or more of the three terms *asti* ("is"), *nāsti* ("is not"), and *avaktavya* ("cannot be expressed"). These are enumerated in the following passage in Dr. Bhandarkar's *Search for Jaina Scriptures* (pp. 95 ff.), to which Jainas often refer for its exposition :—

"You can affirm existence of a thing from one point of view (*syād asti*), deny it from another (*syād nāsti*); and affirm both existence and non-existence with reference to it at different times (*syād asti nāsti*). If you should think of affirming both existence and non-existence at the same time from the same point of view, you must say that the thing cannot be so spoken of (*syād avaktavyaḥ*). Similarly under certain circumstances the affirmation of existence is not possible (*syād asti avaktavyaḥ*); of non-existence (*syād nāsti avaktavyaḥ*); and also of both (*syād asti nāsti avak-*

[1] See *Report of the International Congress of Religions, held at Oxford, 1908;* and the article, *Jainism*, in *Encyclopædia of Religion and Ethics*.

tavyaḥ). What is meant by these seven modes is that a thing should not be considered as existing everywhere, at all times, in all ways, and in the form of everything. It may exist in one place and not in another, and at one time and not at another."[1]

Some Jaina Pandits illustrate the doctrine by pointing out that one and the same man may be spoken of under different relations as father, uncle, father-in-law, son, son-in-law, brother and grandfather.

Decline. From about A.D. 1000 the predominance of Jainism in South India began slowly to wane. This was due to a series of causes. First, the influence of Śaṅkarāchārya, whose inimical teaching gained ground during the ninth and tenth centuries. Second, the fall of the Ganga kingdom of Talkāḍ (1004) and the wide conquests and temporary domination of the Chola kings, who were bitterly hostile to Jainas. Rājendra Chola is said to have ravaged the country as far as Puligere, destroying Jaina temples and monasteries. Third, the conversion of the Ballāl rāja to the Vaishṇava faith about 1100. Fourth, the revival of Vīraśaivism under Basava of Kalyāṇa, about 1160, together with the overthrow of the Kalachuryas (1190). Fifth, the teaching of Madhvāchārya in the thirteenth century, which gave a powerful impetus to Vaishṇavism. Sixth, the rise of the strong Brāhmanical kingdom of Vijayanagar in the fourteenth century. And finally, in the sixteenth century, a wave of Vaishṇava enthusiasm, inspired by Chaitanya preaching the doctrine of Kṛishṇa-bhakti, swept over the peninsula, and completed the alienation of the people from the austere teaching of the Jainas.[2] Despite this change in the attitude of the people, many works continued to be written by Jainas; but their learned men lived in retirement and no longer enjoyed the patronage of courts. In 1838 one of these learned men, named Dēvachandra, of Maleyūr, wrote for a lady of the Mysore royal family a prose work,

[1] Quoted from Mrs. Stevenson's *Heart of Jainism*, p. 92.

[2] On the other hand, the conversion to Jainism of Kumārapāla, King of Gujarāt (1143-73) by the Āchārya Hemachandra, led to a great increase of its power in Gujarāt.

entitled *Rājāvaḷi Kathe*, which is an interesting compendium of Jaina traditions in South India.

THE KAVIRĀJAMĀRGA (850) AND EARLIER WRITERS

The earliest extant Kanarese work of which the date is known is the **Kavirājamārga,** or "The Royal Road of the Poets." This has been frequently attributed to the Rāshṭrakūṭa king, Nṛipatunga, and is commonly spoken of as Nṛipatunga's *Kavirājamārga*. But it is his only in the sense in which the English Authorised Version of the Bible is called King James' Version. Its real author was a poet at Nṛipatunga's court, whose name appears to have been Śrīvijaya. Nṛipatunga ruled from Mānyakhēṭa A.D. 814-877, and was a contemporary of Alfred the Great. The middle of the ninth century, therefore, forms a starting point in the record of Kanarese literature. Whatever was written in Kanarese previous to that date has either not been hitherto recovered, or is not of ascertained date.

The middle of the ninth century, however, is far from being the date of the beginning of Kanarese literature. We have abundant information of a large number of **earlier writers,** extending back into earlier centuries. The *Kavirājamārga* itself mentions by name eight or ten writers in prose and verse, saying these are but a few of many; and it quotes, discusses and criticises illustrative stanzas from other poets whose names are not mentioned. Moreover, the character of the book, which is a treatise on the methods of the poets (see p. 110), itself implies that poetical literature was already of long standing and widely known and appreciated. The author testifies expressly (I, 38, 39), that "in the Kanarese country, not students only, but the people generally have natural quickness in the use and understanding of verse."

In the present chapter such information will be given as is available, not of all, but of the more notable, of these earlier poets, copies of whose works have not yet come to light.

Early Kanarese writers regularly mention three poets as of especial eminence among their predecessors. These are Samanta-bhadra, Kavi Paramēshṭhi and Pūjyapāda. These are apparently not among those named in the *Kavirājamārga*. We are not absolutely certain that they wrote in Kanarese; we know only of their Sanskrit works, Sanskrit being the learned language of that time as Latin was of the Middle Ages in Europe. But inasmuch as they are so uniformly named by later Kanarese writers as eminent poets, it is probable that they wrote in Kanarese also; and what we know of them should be recorded here.

Samanta-bhadra should probably be placed in the sixth century. He was a brilliant disputant, and a great preacher of the Jaina religion throughout India. Pāṭaliputra (Patna), Ṭhakka (in the Panjab), Sindh, Vaidiśa (Bhilsa, in Central India), Karahāṭaka (Karhāḍ in Sātāra district), Vānārasi (Benares), and Kāñchī are especially mentioned as among the places he visited. It was the custom in those days, alluded to by Fa Hiān (400) and Hiuen Tsang (630), for a drum to be fixed in a public place in the city, and any learned man, wishing to propagate a doctrine or prove his erudition and skill in debate, would strike it by way of challenge to disputation, much as Luther nailed up his theses on the door of the church at Wittenberg. Samanta-bhadra made full use of this custom, and powerfully maintained the Jaina doctrine of Syādvāda. It is told of him that in early life he performed severe penance, and on account of depressing disease was about to make the vow of *sallēkhana*, or starvation; but was dissuaded by his guru, who foresaw that he would be a great pillar of the Jaina faith. He is said to have converted Śivakōṭi, the king of Kāñchī, from Śaivism, by some miraculous performance in the Kāñchī temple. Old Kanarese commentaries on some of his Sanskrit works still exist, but of any Kanarese works by him we have no trace.

Pūjyapāda, also called Devanandi, belongs to the sixth or seventh century. He was a Jaina *muni*, or anchorite, who practised yoga, and was believed to have acquired the extraordinary psychic powers which yogis claim. He travelled throughout South India, and went as far as Videha (Behar) in the north. His learning extended over a wide range. He wrote on Jaina philosophy; and also a treatise in Sanskrit on medicine, which long continued to be an authority (see pp. 37 and 45). But his fame rests chiefly on his grammatical works. He not only wrote a commentary on Pāṇini, called *Pāṇini Śabdāvatāra*, but he composed a Sanskrit grammar of his own, entiled *Jainendra*, which obtained great repute (see below, p. 110). One of his disciples, Vajrānandi, is said to have founded a Tamil saṅgha in Madura.

Concerning *Kaviparamēshṭhi* less is known. He probably lived in the fourth century. He may possibly be the same as the *Kavīśvara* referred to in *Kavirāja-mārga*, and as the *Kaviparamēśvara* praised by Chāvuṇḍa Rāya (978) and Nēmichandra (1170), all these names having the same meaning ("eminent poet") and possibly being only epithets.

Whether or not the above trio wrote in Kanarese, there is information about many other writers who certainly did. Among these especial mention should be made of *Śrīvarddhadeva*, called also from his birthplace *Tumbulūrāchārya*, who wrote a great work called *Chūḍāmaṇi* ("Crest Jewel"). It was a commentary on the Tattvārtha Mahāśāstra, and extended to 96,000 verses. Two facts make clear the greatness of this work. An inscription of A.D. 1128 (E.C. II, No. 54) quotes a couplet by the well-known Sanskrit poet, Daṇḍin, of the sixth century, highly praising its author, Śrīvarddhadeva, as having "produced Sarasvati [*i.e.* learning and eloquence] from the tip of his tongue, as Śiva produced the Ganges from the tip of his top-knot." And Bhaṭṭākalaṅka, the great Kanarese grammarian (1604), refers to the book as the greatest work in the language, and as incontestable proof of the scholarly character and value of Kanarese literature. If the author of the couplet quoted is correctly given as Daṇḍin, Śrīvarddhadeva must have been earlier than the sixth century. It is unfortunate that no copy has yet been found of this great work, which appears to have been still in existence in Bhaṭṭākalanka's time.

Other early writers mentioned in the *Kavirājamārga*, but whose works are lost, are *Vimala*, *Udaya*, *Nāgarjuna*, *Jayabandhu*, *Durvinīta* and *Śrīvijaya*. For such fragmentary information as is available of these, the Kanarese student is referred to the *Karṇāṭaka Kavi Charite*. Mention may also be made of *Guṇānandi* (c. 900), quoted by the grammarian, Bhaṭṭākalanka, and always called by him *Bhagavān*, "the adorable"; he was the author of a logic, grammar and sāhitya, *i.e.* a composition in literary, rhetorical style.

Much interest attaches to the name of *Durvinīta*. He was the author of *Śabdāvatāra*; of a Sanskrit version of Guṇāḍhya's *Brihat-Kathā*; and of a commentary on the difficult 15th *sarga* of Bhāravi's *Kirātārjunīya*.[1] He has been supposed to be identical with the Ganga king of the same name, who ruled 482-522. Whether this is so or not will depend partly on the dates of Guṇāḍhya and Bhāravi. Of Guṇāḍhya see p. 38 *note*. Of Bhāravi we only know that he was earlier than 610, when he is mentioned along with Kālidāsa as a famous poet. If he was a contemporary of Kālidāsa, he would belong to the fifth century. Unless he was yet earlier, it is scarcely probable that his work would have been known in South India as early as the date of the Ganga king. Future researches may decide this point.

Although none of the books mentioned in this chapter have yet come to light, some may still be discovered; for there are old Jaina libraries which have been jealously guarded from alien eyes (sometimes buried below ground) and whose contents are not yet fully known.

[1] This *sarga* contains a number of stanzas illustrating all kinds of verbal tricks, like those described in Daṇḍin's *Kāvyādarśa* ("Mirror of Poesy," end of sixth century). *E.g.* stanza 14 contains no consonant but *n* except a *t* at the end (*Na nonanunno nunnono*, etc.); and in stanza 25, each half-line, if read backwards, is identical (*Dēvākā nini kāvādē*, etc.). Macdonell's *History of Sanskrit Literature*.

Stanzas from the Kavirājamārga. A.D. 850

THE KANARESE COUNTRY AND PEOPLE

In all the circle of the earth
  No fairer land you'll find,
Than that where rich sweet Kannaḍa
  Voices the people's mind.
'Twixt sacred rivers twain it lies—
  From famed Godāvarī,
To where the pilgrim rests his eyes
  On holy Kāveri.

If you would hear its purest tone
  To Kisuvōlal go ;
Or listen to the busy crowds
  Through Kōp'na's streets which flow ;
Or seek it in Onkunda's walls,
  So justly famed in song.
Or where in Puligere's court
  The learned scholars throng.

The people of that land are skilled
  To speak in rhythmic tone ;
And quick to grasp a poet's thought,
  So kindred to their own.
Not students only, but the folk
  Untutored in the schools,
By instinct use and understand
  The strict poetic rules. (I. 36-39.)

The original of the first line in the above verses may be quoted as a specimen of the Alliteration, which forms one of the graces of Kanarese poetical composition, but which cannot be reproduced in a translation :

Vasudhā vilaya vilīna viśada vishaya viśēsham.

JAINA WRITERS FROM THE KAVIRĀJAMĀRGA TO THE LIṄGĀYAT REVIVAL (1160)

During the first half of this period, the patrons of Kanarese literature were—in the north, the Rāshtrakūṭas of Mānyakheṭa, and in the south, the Gangas of Talkāḍ. In 973, the Rāshtrakūṭas were displaced by the Chālukyas who made Kalyāṇa their capital. Not long afterwards (c. 1000) the Ganga kingdom, which had lasted for eight centuries, was overthrown by the Cholas. Its power passed, after an interval of Chola domination, to the Hoysalas or Ballāl rājas, who ruled from 1040-1326. The Hoysala capital was at Dorasamudra (Haḷebīd). They are noted for the highly ornate temples they erected.

TENTH CENTURY

The earliest author of whom we have information after the Kavirājamārga was *Guṇavarma I*, who wrote under the patronage of a Ganga king bearing the title Mahēndrāntaka, and therefore identical with Ereyappa, 886-913. He wrote a *Harivaṁśa* or *Nēminātha Purāṇa*, and also a book called *Śūdraka*, in which he compares his royal patron to King Śūdraka, the reputed author of the Sanskrit drama *Mṛicchakaṭikā* or "Clay Cart."

Three poets of the tenth century are sometimes spoken of as the *Three Gems*. These are Pampa, Ponna and Ranna. They are all highly praised by later Kanarese poets.

Pampa, who will be called **Ādi Pampa** to distinguish him from a later poet, was born in 902. He belonged to a prominent Brāhman family of Vengi; his father however abandoned the Brāhmanical faith for Jainism. The son became court-poet, and apparently also a general or minister, under a prince named Arikeśari, who was a descendant of the early Chalukya kings, but at this time was a tributary of the Rāshṭrakūṭas. Arikeśari's court was at Puligere (Lakshmeśvar), and it is in the especially excellent Kanarese of this capital[1] that the poet claims to write. It was in 941, when he was thirty-nine years of age, that the poet composed in a single year the two poems which have made his name famous, and which he says were intended to popularise what to the Jainas were sacred and secular history respectively.

The first book was the *Ādi Purāṇa*, and relates the history of the first Tīrthankara. Mr. Narasiṁhāchārya,

[1] Compare the stanza quoted on p. 29.

than whom there could be no better judge, and who has himself written Kanarese poetry, praises it as "unsurpassed in style among the Kanarese poets."

In his next work, called *Vikramārjuna Vijaya*, but more generally spoken of as the *Pampa Bhārata*, he tells the story of the Mahābhārata. It is interesting as being the earliest extant Kanarese version of this epic. The poet, however, states in his preface that there had been many versions before his. It differs from Vyāsa's account chiefly in the following particulars:—(1) Draupadi is the wife of Arjuna only, not of the five Pāṇḍavas. (2) Arjuna is the chief hero throughout, and it is he and Subhadrā who are finally crowned at Hastināpura. (3) The book terminates at Arjuna's coronation, the later parvas not being included. (4) The poet deliberately identifies his patron, Arikeśari, with Arjuna, and so makes him the real hero. In Oriental style he compares him to Vishṇu, Śiva, the Sun, Cupid, etc.[2] This flattery mars the beauty of the work, although the poem has the advantage of being less Sanskritic in vocabulary than the earlier one. The author was rewarded with the grant of a village.

Contemporary with Pampa was **Ponna,** who, like Pampa's father, was originally of Vengi, and had come into the Kanarese country after his conversion to the Jaina faith. He wrote both in Sanskrit and Kanarese, and hence received the honorific title of Ubhaya-Kavi-Chakravarti ("Imperial Poet in Both Languages"). This title was given to him by his patron, the Rāshṭrakūṭa king, Kṛishṇarāja (called also Akālavarsha and Anupama), who was ruling at Mānyakhēta, 939-968. The poet's fame rests chiefly on his *Śānti Purāṇa*, which records the legendary history of the sixteenth Tīrthankara. It was written at the suggestion of two brothers, who later became generals under a succeeding king, Tailapa, to commemorate the attainment of nirvāṇa by their guru, Jinachandradēva. He was also

[2] We may perhaps compare the way, much less emphatic, in which the English poet Spencer makes Queen Elizabeth the "Gloriana" of the *Faerie Queen*.

the author of the *Jinākshāramāle*, an acrostic poem in praise of the Jinas. Other works attributed to him have not been recovered.

Ranna, the third member of the trio, was a Vaiśya of the bangle-sellers' caste. Mr. Narasiṁhāchārya speaks in high praise of his skill, fluency and fascinating style. He wrote under the patronage of two Western Chālukya kings, Tailapa (973-997), and his successor (997-1008), and from them received various titles of honour. The poet's first work was the *Ajita Purāṇa*, a history of the second Tīrthankara, written in 993. It was composed at the suggestion of a devout lady, the daughter of one of the two patrons of Ponna.

In his second work, *Sāhasa Bhīma Vijaya*, called also *Gadā-yuddha* (the "Conflict with Clubs"), he tells the story of how Bhīma fulfilled his vow to break the limbs of Duryodhana with his club and slay him. But throughout the poem his royal patron, Āhavamalla, whose name lent itself to the comparison, is likened to Bhīma, and becomes the real hero. Other works attributed to this poet have been lost.

Chávunda Ráya, who was the patron of Ranna and a contemporary of the "Three Gems," was himself an author, and in other respects a very remarkable personage. He was a minister of the Ganga king, Rāchamalla IV (974-984), and a general who by bravery in many battles had gained numerous titles of distinction. It was he who at enormous cost had the colossal statue of Gommaṭeśwara executed at Śravaṇa Beḷgoḷa, and it was in recognition of this act of munificence that he received the title of Rāya. He was also a patron of the poet Ranna, and himself has gained a place in the history of literature by a prose work, entitled *Trishashṭi-lakshaṇa Mahā-purāṇa*, but better known as *Chāvuṇḍarāya Purāṇa*, containing a complete history of all the twenty-four Tīrthankaras. The book is of special interest and value because it is the oldest extant specimen of a book written in continuous prose, and therefore enables us to gain a knowledge of the language as spoken in the tenth century. It is dated 978.

About 984 Nāgavarma I wrote the *Chhandombuddhi*, or "Ocean of Prosody," which, with additions by later writers, still remains the standard work on Kanarese prosody. It is addressed by the author to his wife. In the account of the *vṛittas*, each verse is composed so as to be an example of the metre described in it. To him we also owe a Kanarese version of Bāṇa's Sanskrit *Kādambari*, which relates the fortunes of a princess of that name. The author's family had come from Vengi, but he is spoken of as a man of Sayyadi, which is said to be a village in the Kisukāḍu Nāḍ (*i.e.* near Paṭṭadakal ; see map). He states that he wrote under the king Rakkasa Ganga, who was reigning in 984. He also was patronised by Chāvuṇḍa Rāya.

The last three writers were all disciples of the same preceptor, who was also guru to the Ganga king, Rāchamalla.

ELEVENTH CENTURY

In the eleventh century there are not many names of Kanarese writers. This was, perhaps, owing to the disturbed condition of the country caused by the Chola invasions, in which the country was ravaged and many Jaina shrines were destroyed.

In 1049, *Śrīdharāchārya* wrote the earliest extant Kanarese work on astrology, citing the Sanskrit astronomer Āryabhaṭa (499).

To about 1079 belongs *Chandrarāja*, who (apart from the writers of śāsanas) is the earliest Brāhmanical poet in Kanarese literature. He lived under the patronage of Māchi Rāja, a general of the Chālukya king, Jayasiṁha, and for him wrote the *Madana-tilaka*, a short poem remarkable on account of its many ingenious stanzas capable of scansion in various ways, or showing feats of literary manipulation of sounds and words. (See *Karṇāṭaka Kavi Charite*, Vol. I, pp. 74-77.)

To about the same time belongs *Nāgavarmāchārya* of Balipura (Belgāmi, in Shimoga district, capital of the Banavāse 12,000), where he built temples and bathing ghats. He was an Advaitin. His *Chandra Chūḍāmaṇi Śataka* is a cento of verses in praise of detachment (*vairāgya*); it sometimes bears the name of *Jnāna-sāra.*

TWELFTH CENTURY

To about 1105 belongs *Nāgachandra* or *Abhinava Pampa* (the "Second Pampa"), of whom special mention must be made, both for the merit of his style and the unique value of one of his works. Little is known of his personal history; but the statement is probably to be accepted that he was one of a group of poets at the court of the Ballāl rāja, Biṭṭi Deva, the same who afterwards became a Vaishṇava and took the name of Vishṇuvardhana (1104-1141). He wrote the *Mallinātha Purāṇa,* giving the story of the nineteenth Tīrthaṅkara, a work which reveals great descriptive power.

But especial interest attaches to his *Rāmachandra-charitra-purāṇa,* commonly known as the **Pampa Rámáyana,** which was written as a pendant to the *Pampa Bhārata* of his predecessor. This work has unique value, because it preserves for us a Jaina version of the Rāmāyaṇa, which differs in important respects from the Brāhmanical version. While the main thread of the narrative coincides with that of the Vālmīki Rāmāyaṇa, there is a very wide difference in details.

The following are some of the more noteworthy differences:—

The whole atmosphere is Jaina. India throughout appears as a Jaina country. No reference is made to Brāhmans or Brāhmanism. The hermits in the forest are Jaina *yatis.* Rāma, Rāvaṇa and all the characters are Jaina, and generally end their career as Jaina yatis.

The Rākshasas are only occasionally called by that name. They are generally styled *vidyādharas* (*i.e.* beings having the power of movement through the air).[1] In fact, all the inhabitants of the earth belong to one or other of two classes, *khēcharas* (movers through the air) and *bhūcharas* (walkers on the earth), *i.e.* jinns and men.

[1] The hero and many of the characters of the Sanskrit Buddhist drama *Nāgānanda* (seventh century) are represented as *vidyādharas,* literally "possessors of (magical) knowledge."

In place of the supernatural and grotesque marvels of the Brāhmanic story we have a natural and comparatively credible narrative. For example, Sugrīva, Hanumanta and their followers are not monkeys, but human beings whose standard bears the figure of a monkey (*vānara-dhvaja*).[1] No bridge is built across the sea to Laṅka with torn-off tops of mountains; the army is transported across the water through the air by *nabhōgamana vidyā* "as though" on a bridge (XII, 91). Rāvaṇa received the name "ten-headed" not because he really had ten heads, but because when he was born his face was seen reflected on the ten facets of a jewel-mirror which was in the room.

Rāma and Lakshmaṇa are not incarnations of Vishṇu (there is, of course, no horse-sacrifice), but are called *kārana purushas*, *i.e.* beings with a special destiny. They are ultimately identified with the eighth Baladeva and Vāsudeva. Lakshmaṇa is called Kṛishṇa, Keśava, Achyuta. Throughout the wanderings of the exile he is the champion and warrior on behalf of Rāma, and performs all the great exploits; and finally it is by his weapon that Rāvaṇa is slain.

The minor details and episodes differ considerably from the corresponding ones in Vālmīki. For example, Lakshmaṇa and Satrughna have different mothers. Rāma's mother is not called Kausalyā, but Aparājitā. Sītā has a twin brother named Prabhāmaṇḍala, who was stolen in infancy, and only discovered his relationship when wishing to compete for Sītā's hand. Nothing is said of Rāvaṇa's being invulnerable by gods and demi-gods.

Other Jaina versions of the Rāmāyaṇa in Kanarese are the *Kumudēndu Rāmāyaṇa* in shaṭpadi (c. 1275); the *Rāmachandra-charitra* by Chandraśekhara and Padmanābha (1700-1750); and the *Rāmakathāvatāra* in prose by Dēvachandra (c. 1797). The story is also found, more briefly, in *Chāvuṇḍa Rāya Purāṇa* (978), Nayasena's *Dharmāmṛita* (1112), and Nāgarāja's *Puṇyāśrava* (1331), and other works.

There is no equally wide divergence between the Jaina and Brāhmanical versions of the Mahābhārata. The explanation will probably be found in the fact that the Rāmāyaṇa epic grew up in North-East India (Kośala and Videha), the home of Jainism and of Buddism; and is the most famous Brāhmanical outcome of

[1] It is interesting to remember that the standard of the Kadambas of Banavāse, who ruled a great part of the Kanarese country from the third century to 566, was a flag bearing the figure of a monkey, and called *vānara-dhvaja*.

a cycle of floating traditions and legends, which took varying and independent forms, not only among Jainas and Buddhists, but among Brāhmanists themselves. The *Rām-charit-mānas* of Tulsī Dās differs considerably from Vālmiki; so does Kambam's Tamil Rāmāyaṇa. The Buddhists have a *Daśaratha Jātaka*, which makes no mention of Rāvaṇa. The oldest Prakrit poem of the Jainas, the *Paümachariya* (= Padma-charitā) of Vimala Sūri, edited by Prof. Jacobi (Bhavanagar, 1914), and placed by him in the third century A.D., is yet another story dealing with the same characters as the Rāmāyaṇa. The Mahābhārata, on the other hand, belongs wholly to North-West India. Pāṇini, Patañjali, and Amarasimha, who all lived in North-West India, mention the Mahābhārata characters, but never the Rāmāyaṇa characters. Hence there are no Buddhist, and only slight Jaina, variants of the Mahābhārata story.[1]

Other Poets (1100-1160). At the court of the Ballāl Rāja at Dorasamudra at the same time as Nāgachandra were Kanti and Rājāditya.

Kanti is the earliest known Kanarese poetess, and was of the Jaina faith. "Kanti" is the name given to Jaina nuns or female devotees. It is related that the king, to test her skill, made Nāgachandra recite half a stanza, which Kanti would immediately complete; somewhat after a fashion recently current in England of completing "Limericks." A further story, but less probable, is told of how Nāgachandra laid a wager that he would compel Kanti to eulogise him in verse. To effect this purpose he pretended to swoon, and feigned death. When the poetess, struck with sorrow, had pronounced on him a panegyric, he sprang up and claimed to have won his wager.

Rājāditya, a Jaina of Pāvinabāge, is remarkable inasmuch as he devoted his poetical talents to the elucidation of mathematical subjects. With extraordinary skill he reduced to verse rules and problems in arithmetic, mensuration and kindred subjects. His writings are

[1] See *Indian Antiquary*, Vol. XIX (1890), p. 378 ff.

the earliest works on these subjects in the Kanarese language.

Nayasēna (1112) of Muḷugunda, in the Dharwar district, is known by a book on Morals, entitled *Dharmāmṛita*, in which he discourses in easy and pleasant style through fourteen chapters on as many forms of virtue, including courage, truthfulness, chastity, justice, etc. He says in the preface that he has set himself to avoid the needless use of Sanskrit terms, which was a fault of many contemporary poets.

Nāgavarma II (c. 1145) was the author of three important grammatical works, *Kāvyāvalokana*, *Karṇāṭaka-Bhāshā-bhūshaṇa* and *Vastu-kośa*. On these see page 111.

Karṇapārya (c. 1140) wrote, among other works, a *Nēminātha-purāṇa*, or history of the twenty-second Tīrthankara. It includes the stories of Kṛishṇa, the Pāṇḍavas and the War of the Mahābhārata.

Jagaddaḷa Somanātha (c. 1150) translated into Kanarese Pūjyapāda's Sanskrit *Kalyāṇa-kāraka*. This is the oldest extant book on medicine in the Kanarese language. The treatment it prescribes is entirely vegetarian and non-alcoholic.

Vṛitta-vilāsa (c. 1160) made a Kanarese version in champu of a Sanskrit work by Amitagati (1014), entitled *Dharma-parīkshe*. It tells how two Kshatriya princes went to Benares, and in successive meetings with the Brāhmans there, exposed the vices of the gods as related in the sacred books; *e.g.* it is shown that not one of the gods is fit to be trusted with the care of a girl, and the incredibility is urged of such stories as that of Hanumanta and his monkeys. By these discussions their faith in Jainism is confirmed. The work is of value as throwing light on the religious beliefs of the time when it was written. *Brahma Śiva* of Poṭṭaṇagere (c. 1125) is another controversial writer. In his *Samaya-parīkshe*, he points out the defects of rival creeds, and justifies the Jaina position.

Brāhmanical Writers. Beside the *Madana-tilaka* and the *Chandra-chūḍāmaṇi-śataka* already mentioned, the only work by a non-Jaina in this period was a champu version of the *Pañchatantra* by Durgasiṁha (c. 1145). He was a Smārta Brāhman of Sayyadi in the Kisukāḍu-nāḍ, and held office under the Chālukya king, Jagadeka-malla (1139-1149). His work is based professedly on Guṇāḍhya, whom he speaks of as a poet of the court of "Śālivāhana," by which we are probably to understand a Śātavāhana of Paithān.[1]

There were, it is true, other Brāhmanical scholars, but they wrote in Sanskrit. As a rule, their literary work in Kanarese was confined to the composition of *śāsanas* (edicts or deeds of donation, engraved on stone or copper). These are mostly in verse, and often exhibit considerable poetic skill. Special attention may be drawn to the śāsanas dated 929, 1084, 1102, 1137 and 1147, quoted by Mr. Narasiṁhāchārya.

Illustrative Extract from the Pampa Rāmāyaṇa A.D. c. 1105

HOW RĀVAṆA SOUGHT THE AID OF MAGIC IN ORDER TO OVERCOME RĀMA

The following attempt to reproduce, in abridged form, the spirit of a passage in the Pampa Rāmāyaṇa (XIV, 75-105) will serve to illustrate (i) the Jaina atmosphere of the poem; (ii) its serious ethical tone; (iii) the nature of the *champu* style of composition—mingled prose and verse—the verse being of various metres.

Hearing of Lakshmaṇa's perfect recovery from his wound, and of his preparation for a fresh attack, Rāvaṇa's ministers advised him to send Sītā back to her rightful lord, and to make an alliance with Rāma; adding that he could not hope for victory, as Rāma and Lakshmaṇa were stronger than he, and unconquerable. Thereat Rāvaṇa was greatly enraged, and said:

[1] Of Guṇāḍhya's date it is only known that it was considerably earlier than A.D. 600. His *Brihat-kathā*, or "Great Story Book," was written in a "Paiśācha," *i.e.* local Prakrit, language, and is not now extant. But it was the basis of the great collection of stories on Sanskrit, called *Kathā-sarit-sāgara* ("Ocean of Rivers of Story") by Somadeva (c. 1070).

"Shall I, who made e'en Swarga's lord
  Before my feet to fall,
Now meekly yield me,—overawed
  By this mere princeling small?
Nay, better 'twere, if so must be,
  My life be from me reft.
I still could boast, what most I prize,
  A warrior's honour left.

Natheless, to make my victory sure,
  I'll have recourse to magic lore.
There is a spell, the shastras tell,
  Which multiplies the form.
If this rare power I may attain,
I'll seem to haunt the battle-plain.
  My 'wildered enemies shall see,
Before, behind, to left, to right,
Phantasmal Rāvaṇs crowd to fight,
  Whom darts shall strike in vain.
Its name is *bahu-rūpiṇī*.
'Tis won by stern austerity."

That nothing might impede him in the acquiring of his magic power, Rāvaṇa issued orders that throughout Laṅka and its territories no animal life should on any account be taken; that his warriors should for a time desist from fighting; and that all his subjects should be diligent in performing the rites of *Jina pūjā*.

Then entered he the Jaina fane
  His palace walls within.
Attendant priests before him bore
  The sacred vessels, as prescribed
In books of holy lore.
And there to lord Śāntīśvara
  He lowly reverence paid;
Omitting no due ritual
  That might secure his aid.

After worship had been performed with due solemnity, he took a vow of silent meditation; and seating himself in the *padmāsana* posture, began a course of rigorous concentration of mind and suppression of the bodily senses.

And there he sat, like statue fixed;
And not a wandering thought was mixed
  With his abstraction deep.
Upon his hand a chaplet hung,
With beads of priceless value strung,
And on it he did ceaseless tell
The mantras that would serve him well.

When Vibhīshaṇa learned through spies what Rāvaṇa was doing, he hastened to Rāma, and urged him to attack and slay Rāvaṇa before he could fortify himself with this new and formidable power. But Rāma replied :

" Rāvaṇ has sought Jinēndra's aid
 In true religious form.
It is not meet that we should fight
With one engaged in holy rite,
 His weapons laid aside.
I do not fear his purpose fell.
No magic spell can serve him well
 Who steals his neighbour's bride."

Vibhīshaṇa and Aṅgada are disappointed with this reply, and resolve to try and break Rāvaṇa's devotions without the knowledge of Rāma. So they send to disturb him some of the monkey-bannered troops.

They rush toward the town in swarms upon swarms :
They trample the corn, and they damage the farms ;
They frighten and chevy the maidens about ;
And all through the temple they shriek and they shout,
And make a most fearful din.
 But Rāvaṇa stirred not ;—as still as a stone,
 His mind was intent on his *japa* alone.

Then the *yakshas*, or guardian spirits of the Jina shrine, interpose, drive forth the intruders, and appeal to Rāma and Lakshmaṇa to withdraw them. Finally it is arranged that anything may be done to break Rāvaṇa's devotions, so long as his life is not taken and the palace and temples are not destroyed.

Then Aṅgada, heir to Kishkindha's wide soil,
Determines himself Rāvaṇ's penance to spoil.
He mounts on Kishkindha, his elephant proud ;
And round him his ape-bannered followers crowd.
He rides through the suburbs of Laṅka's fair town,
Admiring its beauty, its groves of renown.
He enters the palace, goes alone to the fane ;
With reverence he walks round Śāntīśvara's shrine,
And in lowliness worships the image divine.
When—sudden—he sees giant Rāvaṇa there,
Seated, still as some mountain, absorbed in his prayer !
Surprised and indignant, in anger he speaks :—
" What ! miscreant, hypocrite, villain ! dost *thou*
" In holiest temple thy proud forehead bow—
" Who hast right ways forsaken, thy lineage disgraced,
" The good hast imprisoned, the harmless oppressed,
" And hast snatched from thy neighbour his virtuous wife,—
" How canst *thou* dare to pray in Śāntīśvāra's hall !
" Better think on thy misdeeds, and turn from them all,

"Know by Rāma's keen arrows in death thou shalt fall ;
"And no magical rite the dread doom can forestall.
"When the flames round thy palace leap higher and higher,
"Too late thou digg'st wells to extinguish the fire ! "

Thus saying, he tore off Rāvaṇa's upper garment and smote him with it ; he scattered the beads of his chaplet upon the ground ; he stripped Rāvaṇa's queen of her jewels, and slandered her sorely ; he tied her maidens in pairs by the hair of their heads ; he snatched off their necklaces and hung them round the necks of the Jaina images ; and he defied and insulted Rāvaṇa in every possible way.

The poor trembling women were frantic with fear,
And tried to rouse Rāvaṇ. They bawled in his ear—
"What's the good of thy *japa?* Rise, save us from shame !
"Rise quickly and fight for thine ancient good name."

But Rāvaṇa heard not, nor muscle did move,—
As fixed as the Pole Star in heaven above.

Then a thunderbolt's crash rent the firmament wide ;
And adown the bright flash did a *yakshinī* glide,
And swiftly took station at Rāvaṇa's side.
"I have come at thy bidding," the visitant said,
"I can lay on the field all thine enemies dead ;—
"Save Hanumān, Lakshmaṇ and Rāma divine,
"Who are guarded by might that is greater than mine."

"Alas ! " answered Rāvaṇ, with spirit depressed,
"If those three remain, what availeth the rest ? "

NOTE ON THE DATE OF SAMANTA-BHADRA AND PŪJYAPĀDA.

I am indebted to Dr. J. N. Farquhar for the following valuable information. The chronology of all the early Jaina writers who used Sanskrit and wrote on philosophy depends on the date of Umāsvāti, whose *Tattvārthādhigama-sūtra* is the fountain-head of Jaina philosophy and also of the use of Sanskrit by Jainas. This date cannot be earlier than the fourth century, for he quotes the *Yoga-sūtra*, which cannot be dated earlier than A.D. 300. Samanta-bhadra wrote a commentary on Umāsvāti's great work, and the earliest author who quotes him is Kumārila, who flourished A.D. 700. Thus Samanta-bhadra must belong to the fifth, sixth or seventh century. Pūjyapāda, who also wrote a commentary on Umāsvāti, is placed by the Digambaras between Samanta-bhadra and Akalanka. As Akalanka is attacked by Kumārila, we get this order :—The *Yoga-sūtra*, not earlier than A.D. 300 ; Umāsvāti, fourth or fifth century ; Samanta-bhadra ; Pūjyapāda ; Akalanka ; Kumārila, A.D. 700.

III

JAINA LITERATURE

FROM 1160-1600

In the twelfth century **two new religious movements** showed themselves in the Kanarese country, and thenceforward steadily continued to gain strength. These were Liṅgāyatism, generally represented as originating with Basava in 1160, and Vaishṇavism, originating with Rāmānuja about 1120. The former began at once to affect Kanarese literature; the latter did not influence it to any extent until the fifteenth century. Jaina writers continued to be predominant during the thirteenth and fourteenth centuries, and to hold their own in competition with the others for two centuries more. It will therefore be convenient to continue the account of Jaina literature till the break-up of the Vijayanagar kingdom about 1600. It falls into two periods, corresponding roughly to the times of the later Ballāl rājas and of the Vijayanagar kings respectively.

IN THE TIME OF THE LATER BALLĀL RĀJAS (1160-1326)

Lives of Tīrthankaras. Many of the Jaina works are styled *Purāṇas*, and bear the name of one or another of the Tīrthaṅkaras, whose lives they record. Rarely did a decade pass without one or more considerable works of this sort in champu; as will be seen from the following list:

A.D.	Author	Name of Purāṇa	No. of Tīrthaṅkara
c. 1170	Nemichandra	Neminātha	22
1189	Aggaḷa	Chandraprabha	8
c. 1195	Āchaṇṇa	Vardhamāna	24
c. 1200	Bandhuvarma	Harivaṁśābhyudaya	22
1205	Pārśvapaṇḍita	Pārśvanātha	23
1230	Janna	Anantanātha	14
c. 1235	Guṇavarma II	Pushpadanta	9
c. 1235	Kamalabhava	Śāntiśvara	16
1254	Mahābalakavi	Neminātha	22

It will be noticed that three of the works treat of the popular twenty-second Tīrthaṅkara, who was related to Kṛishṇa. Some of the poets in this list deserve mention for works on other subjects also.

Nemichandra was the author of the earliest known specimen of the Novel, or genuine work of fiction, in the Kanarese language. It is written in the usual champu in a pleasing style, but disfigured by erotic passages. It is entitled *Līlāvatī*, and tells how a Kadamba prince saw in a dream a beautiful princess (the heroine) and she likewise dreamt of him. They were unacquainted, but after mutual search and various adventures were ultimately wedded. The story is based on the Sanskrit romance *Vāsavadatta* by Subandhu (c. 610), but the scene is transferred from Ujjayini to Banavāse.

Nemichandra was eminent at the court of Vīra Ballāla, and at that of Lakshmana-rāja, the Silāhāra ruler of Kolhāpūr. It was at the suggestion of Vīra Ballāla's minister that he undertook to write the *Neminātha-purāṇa*. As the poet died before its completion, it has become known as the *Arddha Nēmi*, the "Unfinished Life of Nēmi."

Janna was a man of varied gifts and considerable munificence, being both court-poet and minister at the Ballāl court, and also the builder and beautifier of temples. He was a pupil of Nāgavarma I. Beside the Purāṇa named above, he wrote several metrical *śāsanas* and also the *Yaśodhara-charitre* (1209). This relates how a king was about to sacrifice two boys of noble birth to Māriamma, but was so moved by their story that he released them, and abandoned the practice of animal sacrifice. Janna's style is highly praised for its grace and dignity.

Bandhuvarma, who belonged to the Vaiśya caste, published (besides the *Harivaṁsābhyudaya*) a well-written book on Morals and Renunciation. It is entitled *Jīva Sambodhana*, because addressed to the *jīva* or soul.

The two poets, *Pārśva-paṇḍita* and *Guṇavarma II*, lived at the court of the Saundatti rājas.

Earliest Sángatya. *Śiśumāyaṇa* (c. 1232) was the earliest poet to write in *sāṅgatya*, a form of composition which afterwards came into much vogue. It is especially intended to be intoned to the accompaniment of a musical instrument. He wrote two books in this style—*Añjanā-charitre*, representing a portion of Ravisheṇa's Sanskrit *Padma-charitrā*; and *Tripura-dahana*, the "Burning of the Triple Fortress," an allegorical poem in which Birth, Decay and Death form the "triple fortress" destroyed.

Ándayya (c. 1235) was the author of a work in champu usually known as the *Kabbigara Kāva* ("Poets Defender"), but also called *Sobagina Suggi* ("Harvest of Beauty"), *Madana-vijaya* and *Kāvana-Gella* ("Cupid's Conquest"). The special literary interest of the work is that it is written from beginning to end without the use of a single unnaturalised (*tatsama*) Sanskrit word, the vocabulary consisting entirely of *tadbhava* (naturalised Sanskrit) and *dēśya* (indigenous) words. It was written at the suggestion of scholars for the express purpose of showing that this could be done; but the example has not been followed since. The subject is the victory of Cupid. Angry with Śiva, who had imprisoned the Moon, he assailed him with his arrows, but was cursed by Śiva to be separated from his bride; but he found means to get release from the curse, and to rejoin his bride.

Mallikārjuna (c. 1245) was brother-in-law to Janna, and father of the Kēśirāja who wrote the *Śabdamaṇi-darpaṇa*. He was a muni and lived in the time of the Hoysala king, Vīra Somēśvara (1234-1254). He compiled the **Súkti-Sudhárnava**, called also the *Kāvya-sāra*, a sort of "Gems from the Poets"—a very useful collection of verses from all previous poets, arranged under eighteen topics, such as descriptions of the sea, the mountains, the city, the seasons, the moonlight, the dawn, friendship, love, war, etc. It contains extracts from works otherwise lost. Only fifteen out of the eighteen chapters have as yet been found. He does not give the names of the poets quoted, but eighteen of them have been traced. A later *Kāvya-sāra*, "Selections from the Poets," was compiled in 1533 by Abhinava Vādi Vidyānanda (see p. 47).

Keśirāja (c. 1260) was author of the well-known standard grammar, **Sabdamanidarpana** (on which see below, p. 111). He came of a very literary family, being the son of Mallikārjuna, the nephew of Janna, and on his mother's side the grandson of another poet, Śaṅkara or Sumanobāna, priest of the Yādava capital, whose works are lost.

Kumudendu (c. 1275) wrote the *Kumudendu Rāmayaṇa*, in shaṭpadi metre (see p. 59). It follows the Jaina tradition, and is largely influenced by the *Pampa Rāmāyaṇa*. No perfect copy, however, has yet been found.

Raṭṭa-kavi (c. 1300), who was the lord of some Jaina town, is of interest because he wrote a quasi-scientific work, entitled *Raṭṭa Mata* or *Raṭṭa Sūtra*, on natural phenomena, such as rain, earthquakes, lightning, planets and omens. It was translated into Telugu by Bhāskara, a Telugu poet of the fourteenth century.

Nāgarāja (c. 1331) wrote in champu *Puṇyāśrava*, fifty-two tales of Puranik heroes, illustrative of the duties of a householder. They are said to be translations from Sanskrit.

Maṅgarāja I (c. 1360) wrote a book on medicine, called *Khagendra Maṇi-darpaṇa*, in which he quotes Pūjyapāda's work on medicine, of the fifth century.

UNDER THE RĀJAS OF VIJAYANAGAR (1336-1610)

Competition with Lingayats and Vaíshnavas. During the Vijayanagar Period, the Jainas had to compete with Liṅgāyats and Vaishṇavas, both of whom were now increasing in numbers and influence. Often debates took place in the presence of the kings between the rival religionists. As early as 1368 the Jainas complained of persecution by the Vaishṇavas; and the king Bukka Rāya, doubtless under the advice of his eminent minister, Vidyātīrtha Mādhavācharya, made them compose their quarrel, and decreed that each party should practise its religion with equal freedom. Copies of this degree are still extant. Nevertheless, the influence of the Jainas was steadily waning.

Lives of Jaina Saints. A large proportion of their writings continued to be the lives of Tīrthaṅkaras, and of other devout and exemplary Jainas. The following are lives of Tīrthaṅkaras belonging to this time:

A.D.	Author	Name of Purāṇa	No. of Tīrthaṅkara
1385	Madhura	Dharmanātha	15
1508	Maṅgarasa	Nemi-Jineśa	22
1519	Śāntikīrti	Śāntinātha	16
1550	Doḍḍayya	Chandraprabha	8
1578	Doḍḍanāṅka	,,	8

Madhura was court-poet of Harihara of Vijayanagar, whose prime minister was his patron. Besides the above work, he wrote a short poem in praise of Gommaṭeśvara of Śravaṇa Beḷgoḷa. Although he belonged to the fourteenth century, he wrote in the scholarly style of the earlier Jaina poets. *Maṅgarasa* was a general of rank. He wrote several works containing stories of Jaina princes.

The life of a pious prince, named Jīvandhara-rāja, appears to have been a favourite subject with the writers of this time. His story was reproduced from the Sanskrit, and told three times over in shaṭpadi—by Bhāskara of Penugoṇḍa (1424), Bommarasa of Terakanāmbi (c. 1485), and Koṭeśvara of Tuḷuva-deśa (c. 1500). Another hero-saint was Nāga-kumāra, a wealthy man who learned to despise riches, and devoted himself to a religious life. His story was told by Bāhubali of Śriṅgēri (c. 1560).

Poets of the Tuluva Country. The next four poets were all from the country below the Western Ghats. It is worth noting that it was during this period that the two colossal Jaina statues in that part of the country were erected—that at Kārkaḷa in 1431, and that at Yēnūr in 1603.

In 1533 *Abhinava Vādi Vidyānanda* of Gersoppa (Bhallātakī-pura), an able lecturer and disputant, who championed Jainism both at Vijayanagar and at many of the provincial capitals, compiled the *Kāvya-sāra*, an anthology of passages on forty-five different subjects from previous poets. It is similar to Mallikārjuna's *Sūkti-sudhārṇava.* As he gives the names of many of the poets, who range from 900-1430, this collection is very useful.

Sāḷva (c. 1550), court poet of a prince named Sāḷva-malla, ruling a city in the Konkan, wrote a Jaina version of the Bhārata known as the *Sāḷva Bhārata.* It was, perhaps, intended to compete with the *Kṛishṇa Rāya Bhārata*, which had been finished not long before, as he bids his readers not to listen to faulty versions, but to follow this pure Jaina narrative. It is in shaṭpadi, and arranged in sixteen parvas, which differ from those of the Brāhmanical version.

Ratnākara-varṇi, a Kshatriya of Mūḍabidire, was the writer of several works. His *Triloka-śataka*, written in 1557, gives an account of the universe (heaven, hell and intermediate worlds) as conceived by Jainas. His *Aparājita-śataka* discourses of morals, renunciation and religious philosophy. His largest work, *Bharat-ēśvara-charitre*, tells the legendary story of the emperor Bharata, who, according to Jainas, was the son of the first Tīrthaṅkara, and became a Jaina yati. Many songs by this author, on moral and doctrinal subjects, are current among Jainas, under the name of *Aṇṇagaḷa-pada*, "Songs of the Brothers."

Nēmaṇṇa, also of the Tuluva country, wrote in 1559 the *Jnāna-bhāskara-charite*, in which he urges that contemplation and the study of the Śāstras are far more valuable for the attainment of emancipation than either outward rites or austerities.

Another poet deserving of mention is *Āyata-varma*, the author of the Kannaḍa *Ratna-karaṇḍaka* ("Casket of Jewels"), a champu rendering from the Sanskrit work of the same name, giving a useful account of the beliefs and duties of Jainas, under the heads of the three Jaina "jewels"—right belief, right knowledge, and right conduct. His date is uncertain. He is conjecturally placed by Mr. Narasiṁhāchārya at about 1400.

IV

THE RISE OF LIṄGĀYATISM

A.D. 1160

Namas tunga-śiras-chumbi-chandra-chāmara-chārave
Trailokya-nagar-ārambha-mūla-stambhāya-Śambhave.

"Adoration to Śambhu (Śiva), adorned with the moon lightly resting like a royal plume upon his lofty head—to Him who is the foundation pillar for the building of the City of the Three Worlds." This, the opening verse of Bāṇa's *Harsha-charita*, is usually placed at the commencement of Śaiva inscriptions.

THE LIṄGĀYAT OR VĪRAŚAIVA RELIGION

The Liṅgāyats are found chiefly in the Kanarese and Telugu countries. They constitute thirty-five per cent. of the total Hindu population in the Belgaum, Bījapur, and Dharwar districts; and ten per cent. in the Mysore and Kolhāpūr States. They call themselves Śivāchārs and Vīraśaivas. The latter name ("stalwart Śaivas") distinguishes them from the three other classes of Śaivas, *viz.* the Sāmānya-, Miśra-, and Śuddha-Śaivas. The first two of these classes worship Vishṇu as well as Śiva; the Śuddha- and Vīra- Śaivas worship Śiva exclusively. That which distinguishes the Vīraśaivas from the Śuddha-Śaivas, and is their most distinctive peculiarity, is the wearing always, somewhere on the person, of a liṅga, *i.e.* a small black cylindrical stone, representing the phallus, but symbolic of the deity. This is worn by both men and women, and is generally kept in a silver or wooden reliquary (*karaḍige*) suspended from the neck. The

Jaṅgamas, or Liṅgāyat "religious," wear it on their head. The investiture with the liṅga is the most sacred rite of childhood. The liṅga is taken out and held in the palm of the hand for worship, but must on no account be parted with throughout life. Liṅgāyats are strictly vegetarian in diet, and on this account all other castes, except Brāhmans, will eat food cooked by them. As they do not admit Brāhman claims to pre-eminence, there is hostility or aloofness between them and Brāhmans. Basava, indeed, taught that men of all castes, and even outcastes, were eligible to enter the Liṅgāyat community.

Other peculiarities are that they do not cremate their dead, but bury them; and that they permit the remarriage of widows; and that every Liṅgāyat is connected with some monastery.[1]

The **scriptures** of the religion are in Sanskrit, and consist of the twenty-eight Śaivāgamas, the earlier portions of which are said to be applicable to all Śaivas, and the later portions to relate especially to Vīraśaivas. There is also an ancient Sanskrit work, called *Śiva-gītā*, to which a high place is given. By the unlearned the *Basava-purāṇa* and *Channabasava-purāṇa* are treated as authorities for their religion; but the learned do not give them this place.

The **leading doctrines** and practices of the Vīraśaiva religion are summed up in the technical terms, *ashṭāva-raṇam*, the "eight environments," or aids to faith and protections against sin and evil; and *shaṭsthala*, the six stages of salvation. As these terms are peculiar to Liṅgāyats, and continually recur in their literature and in the titles of their books, it is desirable to explain their meaning.

The **ashtávaranam,** or aids to faith, are: (1) Obedience to a *guru*; (2) Worship of a liṅga; (3) Reverence for the *jaṅgama* as for an incarnation of Śiva; (4) The devout use of ashes (*vibhūti*) made of cowdung,

[1] See further Farquhar's *Outline of the Religious Literature of India*, pp. 259-64.

which are supposed to have great cleansing and sanctifying power; (5) Wearing of a necklace, or rosary, of *rudrāksha* (seeds of the *Eleocarpus*), sacred to Śiva and a charm of supposed spiritual efficacy; (6) *Pādōdaka*, the washing in, or drinking of, water in which the feet of a guru or jaṅgama have been bathed; (7) *Prasāda*, the presentation of food to a guru, liṅga or jaṅgama, and eating sacramentally what is left; (8) *Pañchākshara*, the utterance of the five-syllabled formula *namaḥ Śivāya* ("Obeisance to Śiva"). With the sacred syllable *Om* prefixed, it is also called *shaḍ-akshara* (six syllabled). Nowadays all these eight safeguards are often combined into a single sacramental ritual at the initiation of a Liṅgāyat child soon after birth.

The *Shaṭsthala*, or six stages of approximation towards union with the deity (Śiva), are termed *bhakti*, *maheśa*, *prasāda*, *prāṇalinga*, *śaraṇa* and *aikya*, the last being absorption into the deity.

The word *Sthala* is also used to denote the eternal, impersonal, divine entity (also called *Śiva-tattva*), which manifests itself further as *Liṅga-sthala* (the personal deity to be worshipped) and *Aṅga-sthala* (the individual soul or worshipper). The three degrees of manifestation of the deity are sometimes described as the *Bhāva-liṅga*, *Prāṇa-liṅga* and *Ishṭa-liṅga*, the first corresponding to spirit, the second to the life or subtile body, and the third to the material body or stone-liṅga.

Reverence is paid to sixty-three ancient saints, called *purātanas*, mentioned also in the Tamil *Periya-purāṇam* and 770 later or mediæval saints (*nūtana-purātana*). Of the former, although all are Śaivas, only eight are Vīraśaivas. Among the later saints are included Basava and his chief disciples. Māṇikka Vāchakar, the famous Tamil mystic (c. 900), is claimed as one of them, and said to be identical with a Mānikayya mentioned among the Śaiva saints in the *Channabasava-purāṇa*.

Liṅgāyatism was the state religion of the early Woḍeyars of Mysore and of Ummaṭūr from 1399-1610, and of the Nāyaks of Keladi (Ikkēri or Bednūr) from 1550-1763. Their principal *maṭha* in the Mysore country is at Chitaldrug.

BASAVA AND THE EARLY APOSTLES OF LIṄGĀYATISM

Basava, the reputed founder of the Liṅgāyat faith, but really only one of its revivers and propagandists, was an Ārādhya Brāhman. According to the traditional account he was the son of Mādirāja and Mādalāmbike. He was born at Bāgavāḍi in the Kalādgi district, but was taken to reside at Kappadi, at the junction of the Malaprabhā and the Kṛishṇa, where there is a shrine dedicated to Śiva under the name of Saṅgamēśvara, "Lord of the Confluence." Here he is said to have become conscious of a call to revive the Vīraśaiva faith. His first wife was the daughter of his maternal uncle, the prime minister of Bijjala, the Kalachuri king, who ruled at Kalyāṇa, 1156-1167. When his father-in-law died, Basava was invited to succeed him as prime minister. The Jainas say that Basava owed his position and influence largely to his having a very beautiful sister, Padmāvatī, whom the king became enamoured with and married; and that the king gave himself up to the charms of his bride and left the reins of power in his minister's hands. Basava had another sister, Nāgalambike, who had a son named Channabasava. In concert with him Basava began to propound his new doctrine and new mode of worshipping Śiva. He speedily gained a large number of followers, and appointed many priests, who were called Jaṅgamas. Having charge of the king's treasury, he spent large amounts in supporting these Jaṅgamas. Bijjala had another minister, a Brāhman, named Manchaṇṇa, who vigorously opposed Basava, and accused him of embezzlement. The king tried to arrest Basava; but he fled, and, being joined by numerous adherents, defeated the king, who was compelled to reinstate him in all his dignities. There was, however, no real reconciliation.

Of what followed there are varying accounts. The Liṅgāyat account is that the king, having wanted to put out the eyes of two Liṅgāyat devotees, Basava pronounced a curse upon Kalyāṇa, and directed one of his disciples to slay the king; and that he then fled to Saṅgamēśvara, and was "absorbed into the Liṅga" (*i.e.* died) there. The Jaina version is that when the king was returning from a military expedition, and was encamped on the bank of the Bhīma River, Basava sent him a poisoned fruit, and then fled to Uḷavi, at the foot of the Western Ghats, where he was besieged by the king's son, and in despair threw himself into a well.[1]

An inscription at Manargoḷi (eleven miles north-west of Bāgavāḍi) of the sixth year (1161) of Bijjala, records a grant to a temple which a Basava had erected there. It gives his lineage, mentioning his father, Chandirāja, and mother, Gangāmbike, as residing at Manargoḷi. It speaks of Basava in very high terms as "without an equal in devotion to Śiva," and as the "virtuous father of the world" who had brought fame to the village. This seems to refer to the Apostle of Liṅgāyatism; but no mention is made of his exaltation to the position of prime minister.

Myths afterwards gathered round Basava's name, and later generations regarded him as an incarnation of Nandi, the vehicle of Śiva, and as having worked numerous and wonderful miracles. All these things will be found written in the *Basava-purāṇa* (1369), the *Mala Basava-rāja-charitre* (c. 1500), the *Vṛishabhēndra Vijaya* (1671), and other works.

To Basava are attributed some prose works expository of the Liṅgāyat faith, *viz. Shaṭ-sthala-vachana*,

[1] The Jaina account is found in the *Bijjala-rāja-charitre* (c. 1650); the Liṅgāyat account in the *Basava-purāṇa* (1369). A later Liṅgāyat account, in the *Channabasava-purāṇa* (1584) absolves Basava from any part in the king's death; but this looks like an apologetic afterthought. A source of information nearer to the time of the occurrences than any of these should be the Telugu *Basava-purāṇa* of Pālkurike Soma (c. 1195), if it is extant.

or "Discourses on the Six Stages of Salvation"; *Kāla-jñāna-vachana*, "Forecasts of the Future"; *Mantra-gopya*, *Ghaṭachakra-vachana* and *Rāja-yoga-vachana*.

Other Apostles of Lingáyatism. As the chief credit of the Liṅgāyat Revival has been universally attributed to Basava, it may be well to state briefly the evidence which shows that he was only one of a number of persons to whom it was due.

(i) Several of his personal associates are expressly named. The chief of these was **Channabasava.** Even in the tradition itself, Channabasava is represented as, in some respects, superior to his uncle. In him the *praṇava*, or sacred syllable *Om*, is said to have become incarnate, to teach the doctrine of the Vīraśaiva faith to Basava; and whereas Basava is represented as an incarnation of Nandi, Channabasava was Śiva himself. As Basava must have been much occupied with affairs of State, the religious portion of the movement may have been, from the beginning, largely under Channabasava's direction. It appears that when, after his uncle's death, he was readmitted to the royal favour, he became the acknowledged leader.

Other leading associates of Basava were Maḍivāla Māchayya, Prabhudeva and Siddharāma. Of these the last-named is mentioned as having made a tank and consecrated many liṅgas at Sonnalige. Of all these early apostles of Liṅgāyatism wonderful stories are told, which are the subjects of the *Channabasava-purāṇa* (1585), the *Maḍivālayya-sāngatya*, the *Prabhuliṅga-līle* (c. 1430), the *Siddharāma-purāṇa* (c. 1165), and other works.

(ii) Frequent mention is made in Liṅgāyat writings of **Five Ácháryas,** whose names are Revaṇa (or Reṇuka), Marula-siddha, Paṇḍitārādhya (or Mallikārjuna), Ekorāmi-tande (or Ekorāma) and Viśveśvarāchārya. The first and third of these belonged to the Telugu country—Revaṇa to Kollipāka (midway between Warangal and Golkoṇḍa), and Paṇḍitārādhya to Vengi. Both of these, as well as Ekorāma, must have been contemporaries of Basava. For it is related of

Paṇḍitārādhya that, after having championed the Vīraśaiva cause at the Choḷa court, he was on his way to visit Basava when he heard of the latter's death. Of Ekorāma it is said that he converted Bijjala's queen; and of Revaṇa that he was the instructor of Siddharāma. The previous incarnations of these āchāryas, referred to in the Basava-purāṇa, may be dismissed as fabulous.

(iii) An inscription of about 1200 at Ablūr in the Dhārwār district records the doings of one, Ekānta Rāmayya, an ardent worshipper of Śiva, who defeated the Jainas in controversy and displaced their temple by a temple to Śiva. He is said to have effected this by laying a wager that he would cut off his own head, and that it would be restored seven days later by the grace of Śiva. Bijjala, hearing of this miracle, summoned him to court, and gave him gifts of land for the Ablūr temple. As these events are placed shortly before 1162, he must have been a contemporary of Basava, but Basava is not named. In the *Basava-purāṇa*, however, which was written 200 years later, it is said that Basava himself was present when the wager was made. It is to be noted that even the śāsana is thirty-three years later than the alleged miracle.[1]

(iv) There were in connection with the court of one of the Ballāl rājas, three Saiva poets, Harīśvara, Rāghavāṅka and Kereya Padmarasa. (See pp. 60, 62.) There has been some difficulty in fixing the particular Ballāl rāja under whom they lived; but Mr. Narasiṁhāchārya has given reason to show that it was probably Narasimha I (1141-1173). If so, they must have been contemporaries of Basava. But they make no reference to him, and must have drawn their inspiration from some other source.

From these considerations it seems probable that the Vīraśaiva movement had already been for some time in progress before Basava; and that the pro-

[1] See *Epigraphia Indica*, v. (1899), *Indian Antiquary*, xxx. (1901), and Bhandarkar's *Vaishṇavism, Śaivism and Minor Religious Systems*, pp. 131-40.

minence which his name has received is due chiefly to the fact that it was his influence at court which gave the movement the political opportunity that led to its rapid dissemination in the Kanarese districts.

THE VACHANA LITERATURE

The Liṅgāyat propaganda was aided by a large number of writers who flooded the country with tracts commending the new creed. These tracts are called *Vachanas*, or "Sentences," and form a unique feature of Liṅgāyat literature. They are in easily intelligible (sometimes even alliterative) prose, requiring no learning to understand. To this fact is doubtless due, in considerable measure, the popularity of the movement. We may perhaps compare the effect produced in England in the fourteenth century by Wycliffe and his preachers and MS. Gospels. In form, the vachanas are brief disconnected paragraphs, each ending with one or another of the numerous local names under which Śiva is worshipped. In style, they are epigrammatical, parallelistic and allusive. They dwell on the vanity of riches, the valuelessness of mere rites or book-learning, the uncertainty of life, and the spiritual privileges of the Śiva-bhakta. They call men to give up the desire for worldly wealth and ease, to live lives of sobriety and detachment from the world, and to turn to Śiva for refuge. They are seldom controversial, but almost entirely hortatory, devotional and expository. They are still recited by Liṅgāyat āchāryas for the instruction of their followers.

Some of the vachanas have a section called ***kāla-jñāna***, which gives a forecast of the future. These portions speak of the coming of an ideal king, named Vīra Vasanta Rāya, by whom Kalyāṇa will be rebuilt and the Liṅgāyat religion come to its full glory.

The vachana literature began in the time of Basava, to whom are attributed six works of this sort; and it continued to be produced through the next three or four centuries. Only a few of the vachanas can be accurately dated, a great number being anonymous. In these cases one author is distinguishable from another only by the divine name which he invokes. Many of the tracts bear identical titles, the most common of which is *Shaṭ-sthala-vachana*.

Specimens of the Vachanas

By Basava

Oh pay your worship to God *now*—before the cheek turns wan, and the neck is wrinkled, and the body shrinks—before the teeth fall out, and the back is bowed, and you are wholly dependent on others—before you need to lean on a staff, and to raise yourself by your hands on your thighs—before your beauty is destroyed by age, and Death itself arrives. Oh, *now* worship Kūḍala-saṅgama-deva.

Those who have means will not devote them to the building of a temple to God (Śiva). Then I, though a poor man, will build Thee one, O Lord. My legs shall be the pillars, my body the shrine, my head the golden finial. Hearken, O Kūḍala-saṅgama-deva! The fixed temple of stone will come to an end; but this movable temple of the spirit will never perish.

The leg does not tire of walking, the eye of seeing, the hand of working. The tongue does not weary of singing; the head does not ache with the binding of the hair; nor does the mind of man desist from desire. Neither shall my heart weary of worshipping and serving Thee, O Kūḍala-saṅgama-deva.

By Uriliṅga-peddi (c. 1180)

Camphor, when touched by fire, itself turns to flame. Salt immersed in water is dissolved into water itself. So the disciple who companions with the True Guru becomes such as the Guru himself. "Like seed, like shoot," is a true saying. Viśveśvara knows—he who is dear to Uriliṅga-peddi.

By Mahādevī-akka

(Of whom it is told that the lord of her city wished to wed her, but she spurned his advances, renounced the pleasures of the world, and went to Kalyāṇa and joined the companions of Basava.)

What sort of a man is he who, having built his house on the mountain, is afraid of the wild beasts there? or, having built it on the seashore, is alarmed by the roar of the surf ? or, if he live in the market street, cannot bear the noise of the traffic ? Then seeing we have been born into the world as it is, we must not be afraid of its praise or its blame, but abstain from passion, and rest unperturbed. Hear my prayer, O Mallikārjuna-deva.

By Swatantra Siddhaliṅgeśvara (c. 1480)

How sadly they fall who are bewitched by the harlot Desire ! Be they ministers or monks, be they scholars or saints, inhabitants of earth or dwellers in heaven, she makes them all to hanker after riches. Who is able to resist her enchantments ? Only those who have found a refuge in the True Guru, Swatantra Siddhaliṅgeśvara. All others she makes to dance at her will.

V

LIṄGĀYAT WRITERS

FROM 1160-1600

Transition from Ancient to Mediæval Kanarese. Whatever the explanation may be, it is a striking fact that the early Liṅgāyat period was marked by important changes both in grammatical usage and in literary form. The letter *ḻa* was entirely dropped, and its place taken by *ḷa* or the half-letter *r*. The letter *pa* at the commencement of a word and in verbal forms was changed to *ha*. And there was a negligence in the observance of the rules of syntax and of rhyme (*prāsa*), which is in marked contrast with the precision of the early Jaina poets. The hitherto dominant champu form of composition, though it still continued to be used by scholars, fell more and more into desuetude. All the metres hitherto used had been those which occur in Sanskrit ; but at this time new and purely Kanarese metres were introduced. These are especially the *shaṭpadi* (six-lined stanzas), the *tripadi* (three-lined stanzas), and the *ragaḷes* (lyrical compositions with refrains). The first to use shaṭpadi was Rāghavāṅka (c. 1165). He was followed, a hundred years later, by the Jaina Kumudendu (c. 1275). A hundred years later still, this metre was adopted in the Basava-purāṇa (1369) and the Padmarāja-purāṇa (c. 1385). It thenceforward became the most common metre of all later works, whether Liṅgāyat or Vaishṇava. Another literary form which dates from this period is the *sāṅgatya*, which appears first in 1232. It became very common after the middle of the fifteenth century.

LINGĀYAT WRITERS IN THE TIME OF THE LATER BALLĀL RĀJAS (1160-1310)

After Bijjala's death the northern part of the Kanarese country (Kuntala) was thrown into disorder. The Kalachuri dynasty succumbed to the Yadavas of Devagiri, whose interests were with the Marāṭhī language. Most of the Kanarese country fell under the sway of the Ballāl rājas, whose capital was at Dōrasamudra (Haḷebīḍ). We now proceed to give an account of the chief Liṅgāyat authors (other than Vachana writers) who lived in the time of these sovereigns.

The earliest is **Harīsvara,** called also Harihara, who was for a time chief revenue accountant of Haḷebīḍ under Narasiṁha Ballāla. He lived for many years under the shadow of the Virūpāksha temple at Hampe, and there he wrote his works. His first was a lengthy book in lyrical (ragaḷe) form, in praise of the sixty-three purātanas and other early Śaiva saints. It is known as *Śiva-gaṇada-ragaḷe*, or from the name of the first saint, *Nambiyaṇṇana-ragaḷe*. He afterwards composed the *Girijā-kalyāṇa*, or "Legend of the Marriage of Śiva and Pārvatī," which gained much popularity. It is written elegantly in the old Jaina style, and is highly praised by all subsequent Liṅgāyat writers. He also wrote *Pampā-śatakam*, a cento in praise of Virūpāksha of Hampe.

Rághavánka was a nephew and disciple of Harīśvara. He was born and lived at Hampe; but he visited and won triumphs at the courts of Dōrasamudra and Warangal, and spent the last years of his life at Bēlūr in the Hassan district. He wrote *Hariśchandra-kāvya*, the legend of the inflexible truthfulness of king Hariśchandra. It is said that his uncle, Harīśvara, was displeased at his having written the praises of a Vaishṇava king, and to make amends he wrote his other works, of which the chief are *Somanātha-charitre*, the history of Somayya of Puligere, whose boast was that he had crushed the Jainas, and compelled them to admit a Śiva image into a Jaina temple; *Siddharāma-purāṇa*, the history of Siddharāma of Sonnalige (See p. 54); and *Harihara-mahatva*, in praise of Harīśvara of Hampe. As already mentioned, he was the first to write in shaṭpadi, the form of verse which afterwards became so popular. An account of him, entitled *Rāghavāṅka-charitre*, was written by Siddha-nañjeśa in the seventeenth century.

Kereya Padmarasa received his prœnomen "Kereya" (tank-builder) through having caused to be made the Bēlūr tank. He was minister of the Ballāl rāja Narasiṁha. When he had retired for some time from this office, and was residing at Bēlūr, he was summoned back to the capital to withstand a Telugu Brāhman, who had come to Dōrasamudra preaching Vaishṇavism. Travelling thither with a company of learned men reciting Śaiva texts, he reached the capital, and so triumphantly vindicated the Vīraśaiva faith that, according to the contract, his opponent had to embrace it. Then he set out, *via* Hampe, on a pilgrimage to Benares, where he died. He wrote *Dīkshā-bodhe*, a volume in *ragaḷe* representing a colloquy in which a guru instructs a disciple and occasionally quotes Sanskrit ślokas in confirmation of Śaiva doctrine. He is the hero of the *Padmarāja-purāṇa*, written by one of his descendants about 1385.

On the date of Harīśvara, Rāghavaṅka and Kereya Padmarasa, see above p. 55.

Kumāra Padmarasa, the son of the last-named writer, was the author of the *Sānanda-charitre*, which tells how a ṛishi's son, hearing of the torments of the lost in hell, attempted to relieve their suffering by the power of the *pañchākshari*.

Pálkurike Soma (c. 1195) was a learned scholar born at Pālkurike in the Godāvari district. After defeating in controversy the Vaishṇava śāstris there, he moved to Kalleya in the Kanarese country, where, both in prose and verse, he praised Basava and the Vīraśaiva faith, and where ultimately he died. His date is fixed by the fact that he is praised by Somarāja (1222); and moreover, according to one account, he was the son of a disciple of Basava. A Telugu *Basava-purāṇa* by him was used by Bhīma-kavi in the preparation of his Kanarese Basava-purāṇa. His Kanarese writings include the *Śaraṇu-basava-ragaḷe* (108 Kandas), the *Śīla-sampādana* (a list of the 64 virtues of Vīra-śaivas), *Sadguru-ragaḷe* and *Channabasava-stotrada-ragaḷe*. He is the subject of the *Pālkurike Someśvara Purāṇa* by Virakta Tōṇṭadārya (c. 1560).

Somesvara-sataka. Some doubt exists as to the authorship of the *Someśvara-śataka*, a popular and widely-read cento of verses on moral subjects. It has by some been attributed to Pālkurike Soma. But Mr. Narasiṁhāchārya says that the work is so loose and faulty, in grammar and style, that it could scarcely have been written by one who, like that scholar, was acquainted with Sanskrit. He also points out that Liṅgāyats themselves do not include it in the list of writings by Pālkurike Soma. Besides which, the author never calls himself Pālkurike Soma, but implies that he belonged to Puligere (Lakshmeśvar). The date of *Puligere Soma* is not certainly known, but he may have belonged to this period.

Stanzas from the Somēśvara Śataka

By Puligere Soma. A.D. 1200. (?)

[As the refrain is capable of being construed in two ways, I have given different renderings of it in alternate verses. Hara and Somēśvara (or Somēśa) are names of Śiva.]

Some facts from professors are learnt,
And some by the śāstras are taught ;
Some lore is the fruit of observing,
And some is arrived at by thought ;
And converse with wise men gives insight ;
And thus to ripe knowledge one's brought.
Many drops coalescing make rivers ;
From rivers the ocean is wrought.
Be Hara, great Hara, adored—
Somēśvara, glorious Lord. (2)

The sun like a jewel adorneth the sky,
The moon like a jewel the night ;

An heir is the cherishéd gem of the home,
  The gems of the lake are the lotuses bright :
The sacrifice' crown is th' oblation of ghee,
  The crown of a wife is her sweet chastity ;
And that which adorneth the court of a king
  Is the presence of poets, fit praises to sing.
    To thee, O Somēśa, I bow ;
    Death's mighty Destroyer art thou. (18)

The moon, though it sometimes is slender,
  Will swell to full roundness again ;
The seed of the banyan, though tender,
  May become greatest tree of the plain ;
The puniest calf to a bullock will grow ;
  The green fruit will ripen in time ;
And so, by the favour of heaven,
  The poorest to riches may climb.
    Be Hara, great Hara, adored—
    Somēśvara, glorious Lord. (45)

What avails it to scrub at your skin,
  If within you are full of foul mire ?
Can the wicked man, clinging to sin,
  By bathing cleanse sinful desire ?
Why, the crows and the buffaloes bathe :
  If to cleanse their beast nature—how vain !
Steep bitter *nīm* fruit in sugar-cane juice :
  Yet it never will sweetness attain.
    To thee, O Somēśa, I bow ;
    Death's mighty Destroyer art thou. (64)

Who waters the forest unbounded ?
  On whose strength do the vast mountains rest ?
And earth, air, fire, water and ether—
  Who but Thou dost with vigour invest ?
Thou alone are upholder of all things that be ;
  And mortals are nought ; they subsist but in Thee.
    Be Hara, great Hara, adored—
    Somēśvara, glorious Lord. (43)

Two Romances. Two authors of this period call for mention as having written books of romance.

Deva-kavi (c. 1200) wrote the *Kusumāvaḷi* in champu. Like the *Līlāvatī* of Nemichandra, it is the story of a prince and a princess who fall in love with one another's portraits, and after many days' search meet and are wedded.

Somarāja (1222), apparently a ruling prince, probably of the Chauta rājas on the West Coast, who had embraced Liṅgāyatism, wrote *Śṛiṅgāra-rasa*, called also *Udbhaṭa-kāvya*. Its hero, Udbhaṭa, the ruler of Gersoppa (Bhallātakī-pura), slays a demon which had been hindering a ṛishi's sacrifice; he then marries the daughter of a Chola king; and in scorn of the thought of going unaccompanied to Kailāsa, like another whom he sees, he lays a wager to take the entire population of the city with him thither.

LIṄGĀYAT LITERATURE UNDER THE VIJAYANAGAR KINGS (1336-1600)

In the time of the Vijayanagar kings who, during two and a half centuries exercised the chief sway in the Kanarese country, literature was being produced by the followers of three religions. The principal Jaina writers have already been mentioned. The Vaishṇava writers will be noticed in a later chapter. An account will here be given of the Liṅgāyat writers only. To enumerate them all would require much more space than this little book can afford. The chief writings may be classified under two heads—Stories of Vīraśaiva Reformers and Devotees, and Expositions of Liṅgāyat doctrine.

Stories of Virasaiva Reformers and Devotees. No religion can make way among the common people if its doctrines are stated only in abstract terms. They must be presented also in the form of biographies, as lived out in the actual experience of men. Therefore, as the Jainas wrote lives of the Tīrthaṅkaras, the Liṅgāyats wrote lives of eminent Śiva-bhaktas.

The first work of importance, belonging to this class, was the **Basava Purána,** written in the shaṭpadi metre by *Bhīma-kavi*, an Ārādhya Brāhman of whose personal life little is known. The book was completed in 1369. It speedily became, and has since remained, a very popular book among Liṅgāyats. Among the authorities on which it is based is mentioned a Telugu work of the same name by Pālkurike Soma.

It professes to tell the story of the life of Basava; who, however, is now represented as an incarnation of Nandī, Śiva's inseparable vehicle, and as especially sent to re-establish the Vīraśaiva faith upon earth. The bulk of the book is taken up with the wonderful miracles Basava performed. The book is an interesting and typical illustration of the mythopoetic tendency, which shows itself more or less in all religions. The method seems to be this. First, a sectarian boast is made in highly hyperbolical terms—such as, that Basava's word is so powerful that by it poison can be converted into ambrosia, the dead restored to life, irrational creatures enabled to confute learned men, mountains can be moved, the sun made to stand still in heaven, a tigress yield herself to be milked. Or else a teaching is recorded in metaphorical language—such as, that those of unclean castes and degrading pursuits are sanctified by the performance, however mechanically, of the powerful Śaiva rites. And then, concrete stories are invented to justify each of these statements. This will give an idea of the kind of miracle (*pavāḍa*) attributed freely to Basava. Finally, Basava is represented as being re-absorbed into the liṅga of the Śiva temple at Saṅgamēśvara.

"As a column of dust raised by the whirlwind arises from the earth, and is lost upon the earth again; as froth is produced in milk when it is churned, and subsides into milk again; as the lightning flash is born of the sky, and recedes into the sky again; as hailstones are produced by water, and melt into water again; so Basava came forth from the Guru and ultimately was re-united with Him in everlasting rest."[1]

Illustrative Extract from the Basava Purāṇa, XI, 9-15. A.D. 1369

BASAVA AND THE KING'S TREASURE

INTRODUCTORY NOTE.—Basava was in charge of king Bijjala's treasury. Just before the time for paying the army, a

[1] An abridged English translation of the *Basava Purāṇa* and *Channabasava Purāṇa*, by Rev. G. Würth, will be found in the *Journal of the Bombay Branch of the Royal Asiatic Society* for 1865-66.

Jaṅgama came along and asked him for the treasure. Whereupon the pious Basava gave him the whole. The king being informed by Basava's opponents, severely reprimanded him, and threatened him with instant dismissal. The poem then proceeds—

But nought perturbed was Basava ;
He calmly smiled and said :—

" Untold, O king, the wealth of him
Who worships Śiva great.
His is the stone Chintāmaṇi
Which finds him all he asks ;
And his the Cow of Paradise,—
The Kāmadhēnu famed ;
The Kalpa-vṛiksha too is his,—
Th' all-bounteous tree of Heaven ;
E'en Meru's golden mount is his :
No good thing can he lack.
What folly then to think that such
Can covet other's wealth !

Will bee that knows the lotus-bloom
A thistle seek instead ?
Will chakōr bird, that has for food
The moon's ambrosial rays,
Exchange that heavenly banquet for
The dark of moonless night ?
Will cub of Indra's elephant
Suck teat of village sow ?

Will *haṁsa*-swan, that's free to drink
Of the boundless Sea of Milk,
Seek salt-sea water for its thirst ?
O Bijjala, bethink !
Or will the lion feed on herbs ?
Will parrot throw away
The mango's luscious fruit to eat
Insipid jungle nut ?
When these things hap, then may'st thou think
The Śiva-bhakta too
May cast his heaven-born treasure down
To steal man's petty gold.

Nay, let the earth reel 'neath our feet,
Great Śesha's head sink down ;
Quenched be the raging fires of Hell,
Splintered the mountain's crown ;
Let moonlight lose its radiance soft ;
The sun rise in the west.
E'en then would he who Śiva knows
Not covet other's pelf.

Does he whose inmost mind doth glow
With heavenly radiance blest
Need man's poor earthen lamp to shed
For him its sickly gleam ?
With thought of Para-Śiva's name
What sweetness can compare ?

Endowed with all the wondrous power
That Śiva-knowledge gives,
I have command of all I wish.
Need I thy money, king ?
Dismiss the doubts that hold thy mind,
And this beside reflect—
That gold was never thine at all ;
'Twas Śiva's—His alone.
Mindful of this, I gladly gave
It all to Śiva Lord.

Yet, mark, O king ! if by my deed
Thou hast a farthing lost,
I've failed to prove a *bhakta* true.
Call for the chests and see."

So the boxes were brought ;
The contents were poured forth.
  Oh the wonder the courtiers saw !
Not a farthing was short ;
The whole treasure was there !
  'Twas most dazzling—that golden store.
The king beamed with delight
At the vision so bright,
  And honoured Lord Basava more.

NOTE.—The above account of one of Basava's alleged miracles, or "signs," shows the ease with which a narrative of professed fact may have grown out of what at first was probably only ethical teaching. It also reveals the consciousness of the possession of valuable spiritual truth which doubtless formed an important part of the dynamic of the Liṅgāyat Revival.

Maha-Basava-raja-charitra is the name of another account of Basava's life, written about 1500 by Siṅgi-rāja, and sometimes called the *Siṅgi-rāja-purāṇa*. It recounts eighty-eight marvellous deeds of Basava, and gives information about his opponents at Bijjala's court.

Later works on the same subject, by Shaḍakshara-deva (1671) and Marulusiddha (c. 1700) will be mentioned in later chapters.

To about the same period as Bhīma-kavi belongs *Padmanāṅka*, another Ārādhya Brāhman (c. 1385), a descendant of Kere-Padmarasa. He wrote the **Padmarája-purána,** in which he extols the victory which his ancestor of 200 years before had won, when he confuted the advocates of other creeds, as related on p. 61.

Prabhuliṅga, also called Allāma-prabhu, is the hero of the **Prabhulinga-lile.** He was an associate of Basava, by whom he was made head of the Kalyāṇa *maṭha* (monastery). He is regarded in this book as an incarnation of Gaṇapati, and it is related how Pārvatī, in order to test the steadfastness of his detachment from the world, incarnated a portion of herself in a princess of Banavāse to tempt him. The author is *Chāmarasa*, an Ārādhya Brāhman. He read his work at the court of Prauḍha Deva Rāya (1419-1446) who highly honoured him, and caused it to be translated into Telugu and Tamil. Chāmarasa was a valiant champion of the Vīraśaivas, and held disputations with the Vaishṇavas in the presence of the king. He was a rival of Kumāra Vyāsa, the author of the Kanarese Bhārata, who had married his sister.

More than a century later, in 1584, when the Vijayanagar court was now at Penukonda, *Virūpāksha Paṇḍita* wrote the **Chánna Basava Purana.** Its hero, Chānnabasava, is regarded as an incarnation of Śiva. The work relates his birth, and his greatness at Kalyāṇa; but is mostly taken up with the instruction he gave to Siddharāma of Sonnalige on the entire body of Vīraśaiva lore—the creation, the wonderful deeds (*līle*) of Śiva, the marvellous efficacy of Śaiva rites, and stories of Śaiva saints. It has consequently been very popular among Liṅgāyat readers. It is also very useful to the historian of Kanarese literature, because it gives much help in determining the approximate dates of the early Vīraśaiva saints and poets. The book closes with a prophecy that Vīra Vasanta Rāya would come and rule the Kanarese country in 1584, and rebuild and beautify Kalyāṇa. It thus identifies Vīra Vasanta Rāya with

Veṅkaṭapati Rāya, who ascended the throne in that year.[1]

There are also **lives of Ácháryas and Purátanas.** The most popular of the Āchāryas was **Panditárádhya.** His story had been already told by Pālkurike Soma both in Telugu and Kanarese, and by Guru-rāja (c. 1430) in Sanskrit. It was now retold in Kanarese in the *Ārādhya-charitra* of Nīlakaṇṭhāchārya of Ummaṭūr (c. 1485) and by Mallikārjuna-kavi (1593) in a commentary on Guru-rāja's Sanskrit work. **Revana Siddha,** another Āchārya, had his story told before, not only in Sanskrit, but also by Harīśvara in Kanarese. It was now retold in Mallaṇṇa's *Rēvaṇa-Siddheśvara-kāvya* (1413) and in Chaturmukha Bommarasa's *Rēvaṇa-Siddhesvara-purāṇa* (c. 1500). The latter author was a disciple of a descendant of Rēvaṇa. A later work, *Chaturāsya-purāṇa* (1698) gives the lives of all the Āchāryas except Viśveśvara.

Concerning the *purātanas* we have the following:

Author	*Date*	*Name of Work*	*Subject*
Bommarasa ..	c. 1450	Saundara-purāṇa	Nambiyaṇṇa
Nijaguṇa-yogi	c. 1500	Purātanara-tripadi	63 purātanas
Suraṅga-kavi (of Puligere)	c. 1500	Trishashṭi-purātanara-charitre (champu)	,,
Gubbi Mallanārya ..	1513	Vīraśaivāmrita-purāṇa	Purātanas and others
Virupa-rāja ..	1519	Tribhuvana-tilaka (sāṅgatya)	King Cheramāṅka
Kumāra-Channabasava	c. 1550	Basava-purāṇada-purātanara-charitre	Purātanas and others

Works expository of Virasaiva doctrine. Of the numerous works of this character only a selection can

[1] Veṅkaṭapati Rāya's father, Tirumala Rāya, had done much to restore the prestige of the dynasty after the disastrous defeat of Taḷikōṭa and the fall of Vijayanagar. Among the many successes which he claims in inscriptions is the defeat of the Raṭṭas, and he accordingly styles himself "Lord of Kalyāṇapura." This fact is probably the ground of the poet's hopeful forecast. But as a matter of fact, Kalyāṇa remained in the territory of Bijapur until that State was annexed by the Mughal Emperor. The prophecy must be taken therefore as a piece of courtly flattery.

here be named. For the most part, commentaries on Sanskrit works will not be mentioned at all.

The **reign of Praudha Deva Râya** (1419-1446) seems to have been a time of much literary activity. Two of his ministers were zealous in the propagation of Liṅgāyat doctrine. One, named *Lakkaṇṇa*, wrote a treatise on the beliefs and religious rites of the sect, entitled *Śivatattva-chintāmaṇi*, "Handbook of Śaiva Doctrine." Another, named *Jakkanārya*, not only himself wrote, or reproduced from the Sanskrit, a work entitled *Nūrondu-sthala* ("Hundred and One Topics"), but spent large sums on the composition of Liṅgāyat works by other scholars. The chief of these scholars were Kumāra-baṅka-nātha and Mahāliṅga-deva. Both of them were eminent gurus of the time; and both wrote Vachanas and books on the Shaṭ-sthala. The former also wrote a *Śivatattva-chintāmaṇi*.

Guru Basava, another eminent guru, was the author of seven works, called the *Sapta-kāvya* (or "Seven Classics"), all of which expounded religious teaching in the form of colloquys between a guru and his disciple. All are in shaṭpadi, except the *Avadhūta-gīte*, which consists of songs in praise of detachment.

Mention is also frequently made of a *hundred and one Viraktas*, or teaching Jaṅgamas, who lived during the same king's time. Several of these wrote Vachanas and works on the Shaṭ-sthala. The principal were Kalmaṭha Prabhudeva, who wrote in prose, and Karasthala Nāgideva.

There was great rivalry at the time between Liṅgāyats and Vaishṇavas. Each in turn organised processions through the town in honour of the books of their respective faiths. Chāmarasa and Kumāra Vyāsa, both mentioned elsewhere (pp. 68, 78), are especially noticed as rivals. This rivalry is further illustrated by the *Prauḍha-rāyacharitre* of Adṛiśya (c. 1595), which consists of stories of Śaiva saints, represented as told to this king by Jakkanārya in order to turn his mind from listening to the Bhārata, and to convince him of the superiority of Liṅgāyatism.

In the reign of Virūpāksha (1467-1478) there lived a guru named **Tonṭada Siddhesvara** or **Siddhalinga-yati** who had a very large number of disciples and exercised a wide influence. He derived his prœnomen Tōṇṭada ("garden") from the circumstances that he long practised Śiva-yoga in a garden on the bank of the Nāginī river near Kaggere. He was buried at Yeḍiyūr, near Kunigal, where a *maṭha* was built in memory of him, and where a temple in his honour still exists. All succeeding Liṅgāyat writers speak his praise. He wrote a prose work of 700 vachanas, entitled *Shaṭsthala-jñānāmṛita*. One of his vachanas has been quoted above. Several of his disciples were authors of similar works. His history is recorded in the *Siddheśvara-purāṇa* by Virakta Tōṇṭadārya (c. 1560).

Nijaguna-siva-yogi lived at some time between 1250 and 1655. His date cannot at present be more accurately given, but he falls somewhere within the period which we are considering. He was a great scholar and a prolific writer. He was the ruler of the country round Śambhuliṅga hill near Yelandūr, and finally retired to that hill and lived there as a Śiva-yogi. In all his works he extols Śambhuliṅga. He did not write, like the others, in shaṭpadi, but employed tripadi, sāṅgatya, ragaḷe and prose. One work is a commentary on the Sanskrit *Śiva-yoga-pradīpikā*, written especially for the benefit of those ignorant of Sanskrit who desire emancipation. But his best know work is the *Viveka-chintāmaṇi*, a very useful encyclopaedia of Sanskrit terms and Vīraśaiva lore.

Mallanárya of Gubbi was a learned man who lived in the reign of Kṛishṇa-deva-rāya (1509-1529). He wrote both in Kanarese and Sanskrit. He is chiefly known by two works. His *Bhāva-chintāratna* (1513) is a reproduction in Kanarese shaṭpadi of a Tamil work by Jñāna-sambandhar (Pillai Naynār) of the seventh century. It is sometimes called the *Satyendra-Chola-kathe*, because it tells a story of the Choḷa king which was designed to illustrate the power of the *pañchāksharī*. The same story was, at a later date, elaborated in the more famous *Rājaśekhara* of Shaḍaksharā-deva (see p. 84). The other work, *Vīraśaivāmrita* (1530), also in shaṭpadi, gives a full statement of Liṅgāyat beliefs and traditions, supporting its teaching by quotations from the sacred books. It describes Śiva's twenty-five *līles* (or "sports") and gives stories of the purātanas and their successors. Like many other doctrinal works, it is put in the form of instruction given by a guru to his disciple.

Virupa-rāja and *Vīrabhadra-rāja* were two writers of princely lineage. The former has already been mentioned (p. 69). Vīrabhadra-rāja was his son, and wrote five śatakas on Vīraśaiva doctrine and morals.

At the close of this period I will place a poet whose date is not yet decisively ascertained. This is **Sarvajna-múrti,** the composer of the *Sarvajña-padagaḷu*, very popular verses in tripadi metre, embodying much shrewd wisdom, and frequently quoted by the common people. Sarvajña is one of those poets whose artless and casual verses so express the better thoughts, which the common people feel but cannot express, that they have become the property and favourites of all, and are loved and quoted alike by ryot and tradesman and wandering mendicant. His real name was Pushpadatta. He tells us that he was the son of a Śaiva Brāhman of Māsūr, in the Dhārwār district, by a widow named Māḷi, whom his father met in a potter's house at Ambalūr, while he was on his way home from a pilgrimage to Benares. About a thousand of his verses are current. Various collections of these have been made. Of the printed copies no two are exactly alike; and these probably include a few verses which imitators have added later. The subjects, which are arranged under 47 or 49 heads, are chiefly religion, morals and society; but there are also verses on astrology, weather-lore, etc., and even riddles. Sarvajña occupies much the same place in Kanarese literature that Vēmana does in Telugu, and Nām-dev (fourteenth century ?) and Tukā Rām (d. 1649) do in Marāṭhī. Like them he preached the vanity of idol-worship, the inefficiency of pilgrimages and of outward rites, and the need of sincerity in life.

The following is the evidence as to his date:—(1) Collections of his verses have been found, written earlier than 1800; which proves that a verse in which he is made to foretell the fall of Seringapatam (1799), and probably another in which he speaks of that of Ikkēri (1763) are not authentic. (2) His use of the letter *ṛa* shows that he cannot have been later than 1700; and the old Kanarese grammatical forms which he employs confirm this judgment. (3) One palm-leaf manuscript found by Mr. Narasiṁhāchārya states that the collection was made by Sampādaneya Siddhavīrāchārya, who is known as a diligent compiler of Vīraśaiva verses and prose *vachanas*, and who lived somewhere about 1600. This would place Sarvajña in the sixteenth century. Mr. Narasiṁhāchārya, while stating these facts, places him about 1700.

Verses by Sarvajña. (A.D. 1600?)

NOTE.—The terseness of Sarvajña's verses can scarcely be reproduced in a Western language except at the cost of clearness. The following renderings only represent the sense. The poet appends his name to every stanza, much as an artist signs every sketch he makes.

CASTE

When light enters Pariah dwelling, is *it* also outcaste for that?
Oh, talk not of "high caste" and "outcaste."
The man on whose homestead God's blessing doth shine
Is surely a noble of lineage divine. Sarvajña.

We all tread the same mother earth;
The water we drink is the same;
Our hearth-fires glow no distinction doth show;
Then whence cometh caste, in God's name? Sarvajña.

FATE

They say that Lord Vishṇu once lived as a boar;
That Śiva went begging from door to door;
The Brahmā himself had his head cut away,
Who was it that settled *their* destiny, pray? Sarvajña.

IGNORANT WORSHIP

The foolish who bow to a wayside stone,
And are not aware of the One God alone—
These we should only for Pariahs own. Sarvajña.

VAIN PILGRIMAGE

Why seek for THE GOOD on a distant shore?
Look! meanwhile it grows at your own house door! Sarvajña.

VI

THE RISE OF VAISHNAVA LITERATURE

1500-1600

Jayaty-āvishkṛitam Vishṇor varāham kshobit-ārṇavam
Dakshiṇonnata-daṁshṭrāgra-viśrānta-bhuvanam vapuḥ.

"SUPREME is the boar form of the resplendent Vishṇu, which scattered the waters of the ocean and raised up the peaceful earth on the tip of his long right tusk."

This couplet usually heads Vaishṇava inscriptions.

THE VAISHṆAVA REVIVAL

The Vaishṇava Revival was a revolt against the unsatisfying character of the *advaita* teaching of Saṅkarāchārya. For three hundred years after Śaṅkarāchārya's time, *i.e.* from 800-1100, his presentation of monism and his doctrine of illusion (*māyā*) had held the field of philosophic teaching and dominated the religious thought of the people, unchallenged from within Hinduism. But that system had reduced God to a pure abstraction, an unconscious entity, which could not satisfy man's craving for worship, sympathy and communion. The Vaishṇava reformers strenuously contended against the interpretation put upon the Upanishads by the Illusionists (*māyā-vādīs*), as they called Śaṅkara's followers. Accepting the same books as authorities, they gave them a new interpretation, and taught that the Supreme, the "One only without a second," was a deity with a personality—a Being to stir, and respond to, devotion, reverence and love.

The two great Reformers who initiated the movement were Rāmānujāchārya, early in the twelfth century, and Madhvāchārya,[1] in the thirteenth century. Of these, the former, whose centre was at Śrīraṅgam, was driven by persecution into the Kanarese country, where he converted the Ballāl rāja from Jainism, and established the important *maṭha* of Mēlkōṭe. His works are in Sanskrit; those of his followers chiefly in Tamil. The second was born and lived in the Kanarese country, with Uḍupi as his centre, and although he himself wrote in Sanskrit, he inspired many works in Kanarese. The followers of Rāmānuja are called Śrī Vaishṇavas, and worship Vishṇu exclusively; the Mādhvas worship Vishṇu chiefly, but not to the exclusion of Śiva.

It is worthy of note that the revolt against the teaching of Śaṅkara was shared by Śaivas also; and the feeling that they had a common cause led, during the twelfth, thirteenth and fourteenth centuries, to various attempts being made to reconcile the rival Vaishṇava and Śaiva creeds, by building temples to a combined deity, called Harihara or Śaṅkara-Nārāyaṇa.[2] But the most important fact is that, whether the deity worshipped was called Vishṇu (Hari) or Śiva (Hara) or Harihara, he was conceived of as *personal*, and not as abstract; so that *bhakti* (ardent personal devotion) took the place of *tapas* (austerities, self-mortification) and of *yogābhyāsa* (self-hypnotism).

The personal Śiva has been ardently worshipped in the Tamil country, but, speaking generally, has never called forth personal devotion to the same extent as the more human incarnations of Vishṇu in Rāma and Kṛishṇa. In North India, through the teaching of Rāmānanda, (fifteenth century) followed up by Kabīr (1440-1518) and

[1] Madhvāchārya is sometimes by European writers confounded with Mādhavāchārya (the author of the *Sarvadarśana Saṅgraha*, the brother of Sāyana, and minister of Bukka Rāja in the fourteenth century).

[2] Witness the Śaṅkara-Nārāyaṇa temple at Dāvaṅgere, mentioned in a grant of 1147; the temple to Harihara, erected 1223 (hard by which the agrahāra of Harihara was established in 1418); and the name Harihara, borne by the first Vijayanagar king (1336-53), by others of his line, and by the poet Harīśvara (c. 1165).

Tulasi Dās (1532-1623), the new cult of Rāma rapidly spread, of the existence of which there is no clear evidence before about the eleventh century.[1] In South India, Rāmānuja and Madhvāchārya adhered to the already existing cult of Kṛishṇa, as he is represented in the Mahābhārata, which (except in interpolated passages) makes no mention of the stories of Kṛishṇa's boyhood or of his sports with the gōpīs. This element, however, soon came in through the popularity of the Bhāgavata Purāṇa, which, in its original Sanskrit form, dates from about the ninth or tenth century.

In addition to the reason already given, the Vaishṇava Revival owed its success to its drawing freely from the rich stores of attractive legend contained in the Sanskrit Epics and the Bhāgavata—to its extensive use of song and kīrtan—to its large *māhātmya* literature—and also doubtless to the less austere character of its chief hero.

VAISHṆAVA LITERATURE TO 1600

Early Vaishnava Works. Actually the earliest Vaishṇava writer of importance in Kanarese would seem to be *Rudrabhaṭṭa*, a Smārta Brāhman, of the time of Vīra Ballāla (1172-1219), and author of the *Jagannātha Vijaya*, which reproduces in champu the narrative of the Vishṇu Purāṇa, from the birth of Kṛishṇa to his fight with Bāṇāsura.

Another early writer was Narahari-tīrtha of the Uḍupi maṭha, third in succession from Madhvāchārya. In 1281 he wrote, in Kanarese, songs in praise of Vishṇu. Before becoming a sannyāsī, he had been an official in Ganjam, where two śāsanas composed by him have been found. He is said to have died in 1333.

It was not, however, till the period of the Vijayanagar kingdom and the reign of Kṛishṇa Rāya (1509-29) that

[1] See Sir R. G. Bhandarkar's *Vaishṇavism and Śaivism*. Rāma had indeed been recognised as an *incarnation* of Vishṇu several centuries earlier ; but there is no evidence that separate temples had been erected in his name. But see also Dr. J. N. Farquhar's *Religious Literature of India*, pp. 189 f., 249 f.

the Vaishṇava movement made itself strongly felt in Kanarese literature.

It is at this time, the sixteenth century, and especially in the poetry of the Vaishṇavas, that a **transition from Mediæval to Modern Kanarese** begins to take place. This shows itself in the following among other ways:—Many ancient verbs and nouns fall into disuse (perhaps because of their association with a different school of religious thought). The letter *ṟa* begins to be used laxly in alliteration with other letters, and is finally dropped altogether. Verbs, nouns and suffixes hitherto having consonantal endings, now have the vowel *u* added to them to assist enunciation. The form of the present tense is changed, and a contingent future is newly introduced.[1]

Translations of Sanskrit Classics. Vaishṇava Kanarese literature consists very largely of reproductions, in various forms, of Sanskrit works. The progress of the Vaishṇava movement was considerably helped in the early years of the sixteenth century by the publication in rapid succession of Kanarese shaṭpadi versions of its three great classics.

The first to appear was the leading story of the Mahābhārata, in which Kṛishṇa, identified with Vishṇu, is the great hero. Of this, the first ten parvas had already been translated by Nāraṇappa, a Brāhman gauḍa or śānabhōg of Kōdivāla in the Dharwar district, but better known by his *nom-de-plume*, Kumāra Vyāsa. Liṅgāyat writers mention that he was a rival of Chāmarasa, the author of the *Prabhuliṅgalīle*, and married his sister. He must, therefore, have lived in the reign of Prauḍha Deva Rāya (1419-46). As his work is dedicated to the deity at Gadag, it is often called the **Gadugina Bhárata.** The author, however, died before he could complete his task. The remaining parvas (from Śānti onwards) were added about 1510 by Timmaṇṇa, who describes his work as blending with that of Kumāra Vyāsa, as the waters of the Jumna with those of the

[1] Kittel's *Kannaḍa-English Dictionary* (Preface), and his *Grammar of the Kannaḍa Language*.

Ganges. His work was entitled, after his royal patron, the *Kṛishṇa-rāya Bhārata.*

The success of the Bhārata led to a similar presentation of the story of the Rāmāyaṇa, which was now given to Kanarese readers for the first time from the Brāhmanical standpoint. The work was produced at Torave, in the Sholapur district, and is generally known as the **Torave Rámáyana.** The author calls himself *Kumāra Vālmīki*, after the author of the Sanskrit Rāmāyaṇa; but his real name was Narahari. His exact date is unknown; but it is later than Kumāra Vyāsa, whom he mentions. Mr. Narasiṁhāchārya places him about 1500; but no mention of him seems to have been found till the eighteenth century.

The **Bhágavata Purána** was the third great Vaishṇava classic reproduced in Kanarese about the same time. Its author was Chāṭu-Viṭṭhala-nātha, who appears to have lived at Vijayanagar in the time of Kṛishṇa Rāya and Achyuta Rāya. His date is about 1530. He also prepared a fuller rendering of the Pauloma and Āstīka parvas of the Mahābhārata, which had only been briefly summarised by Kumāra Vyāsa.

It will be observed that the three great Vaishṇava classics were probably all completed during the reigns of Kṛishṇa Rāya (1509-29) and Achyuta Rāya (1530-42). This was a period in which the literatures of Kanarese and Telugu meet, both languages being equally patronised by these princes, who are said to have had eight celebrated poets at their court. Beside the Vaishṇavas just mentioned, there were, among those who flourished at the same time, the Liṅgāyat Mallanārya, and the Jainas, Maṅgarasa and Abhinava Vādi Vidyānanda.

Popular Devotional Songs. The worship of Kṛishṇa was further popularised by short songs in *ragaḷe* metres by Vaishṇava *dāsas*, or mendicant singers, who wandered from village to village. They received their inspiration from Madhvāchārya, to whom they all express indebtedness, and from Chaitanya, who, about 1510, visited all the chief shrines of South India, teaching men everywhere to chant the name of Hari, and who died at Puri in 1533. A collection of 402 of these devotional songs in Kanarese was made by Rev. Dr. Moegling, who published 174 of them in Mangalore in 1853, and these have since been reprinted in Bangalore. They are known as the **Dásara Padagalu.**

The earliest, most prolific and most famous of the singers was **Purandara Dása**, who lived at Paṇḍharpur, and visited Vijayanagar in the time of Achyuta Rāya. It is said that as a young man he was rich and close-fisted; but afterwards gave away his possessions, and lived as a mendicant, singing the praises of Vishṇu in Paṇḍharpur, where he died in 1564. All his songs end with the name Purandara Viṭṭhala.[1]

A contemporary of his was of **Kanaka Dása,** of Kāginele in the Dharwar district. He was of the *bēḍa* (hunter) caste, or, as some say, a *kuruba* (shepherd). Like Purandara, he owed his change of life to Vyāsa-rāya, the head of the Mādhva maṭha at Sosile, who himself composed lyrics in praise of Kṛishṇa. Beside hymns extolling Vishṇu, Kanaka Dāsa wrote, in sāṅgatya, the *Mohana-taraṅginī* ("River of Delight," consisting of Purāṇic stories chiefly about Kṛishṇa) ; and, in shaṭpadi, a *Nala-charitre* and a *Hari-bhakti-sāra*. This last, which treats of morals, devotion and renunciation (*nīti*, *bhakti*, *vairāgya*), has long been in popular use as a book for children to learn.

There exists a pretty little poem of fancy by Kanaka Dāsa, entitled *Rāma-dhānya-charitre* ("The Story of Rāma's Chosen Grain"), in which he invents an ingenious, and characteristically religious, derivation for the word *rāgi*, which is the name of the staple food of a great part of the Kanarese country. The poem says that, after the death of Rāvaṇa, Rāma visited a hermitage, and enjoyed the food set before him by the ascetics. He then proposed for discussion the question—"Which of all the grains is most excellent?" The claims of rice being disputed by another grain, known as *naredalega*

[1] *Viṭṭhala* and *Viṭhobā* are corrupt Kanarese forms of *Vishṇu* (Viṭṭhu) with the affixes *la* and *bā* to denote tenderness or reverence. (Dr. Bhandarkar.)

("grey-head"), the gods came down to investigate the case. After hearing the arguments on both sides, Indra decided in favour of *naredalega*. Whereupon Rāma conferred upon it his own royal name of *rāghava*; whence its present name of *rāgi*![1]

The names of other singers are Viṭṭhala Dāsa, Veṅkaṭa Dāsa, Vijaya Dāsa, and Kṛishṇa Dāsa, the last three all being of Uḍupi. Along with these may be mentioned Varāha Timmappa Dāsa, who was only less prolific than Purandara Dāsa and Kanaka Dāsa; but he lived two centuries later, in the time of Haidar Ali. When Sāgar fell into the hands of Haidar, he fled to Tirupati. Contemporary with him was Madhva Dāsa, of Uḍupi.

The chief object of the poems is to extol Vishṇu above all other gods, and exhort men to worship him. The gist of one of the songs is—"There is no god equal to Vishṇu; no tīrtha equal to the Śāligrām; no book equal to the *Bhārata*; no life-force (*chaitanya*) equal to Vāyu; no teaching equal to that of Madhva; no caste equal to the Brāhman caste." They record the exploits of Kṛishṇa and commend pilgrimages to his shrines. They also give expression to weariness of the world, the sense of sin and helplessness, a depreciation of outward rites and a yearning after purity and divine help; and, warning men of the approach of death and the penalties of hell, call them to a religious life. Mr. Charles Gover, in his *Folk Songs of Southern India*, has given a free translation into English verse of twenty-eight of these songs. Of these I quote one by Purandara Dāsa.

[1] In *J.R.A.S.*, July, 1920, Mr. Havell gives reasons for identifying *rāji* with the plant from which *soma*, the sacrificial drink of the original Āryan Brāhmans, was made. If this can be substantiated, it is of much interest.

A Song in Praise of Vishṇu

BUY MY SUGAR-CANDY (THE NAME OF HARI)

My stock is not packed on the backs of strong kine ;
Nor pressed into bags strongly fastened with twine.
Wherever it goes it no taxes doth pay
But still is most sweet, and brings profit, I say.

Refrain: Oh buy sugar-candy, my candy so good,
For those who have tasted say nought is so sweet
As the honey-like name of the godlike Vishṇu.

It wastes not with time ; never gives a bad smell ;
You've nothing to pay, though you take it right well ;
White ants cannot eat the fine sugar with me ;
The city resounds as its virtue men see.

From market to market 'tis needless to run ;
The shops know it not, the bazaar can have none.
My candy, you see, is the name of Vishṇu,
So sweet to the tongue that gives praise as is due.

Another work popularising the worship of Kṛishṇa was the *Hari Bhakti Rasāyana* ("Elixir of Devotion to Vishṇu"), by Chidānanda, of the eighteenth century.[1]

[1] There exists also a Śaiva (not Vīraśaiva) *Bhakti-rasāyana* in shaṭpadi by Sahajānanda, a Smārta, of the seventeenth century.

VII

KANARESE LITERATURE IN THE XVII AND XVIII CENTURIES

DURING the seventeenth century the Vijayanagar Empire broke up into many small states, or pāḷayagāris, each vassal chieftain declaring his independence. The Mysore State gradually absorbed many of these, and finally emerged as the dominant power in the southern part of the Kanarese country.

THREE OUTSTANDING WORKS

In the seventeenth and early in the eighteenth century there were three writers who deserve especial mention, as each produced something eminent in its own department. They belong to each of the three chief faiths of the people—one a Jaina, another a Liṅgāyat and the third a Vaishṇava Brāhman; and they were all independent of royal patronage.

The first was *Bhaṭṭākalaṅka Deva*, a disciple of the Jaina guru of the Haḍuvalli *maṭha*, in South Kanara. He was an accomplished scholar in both Sanskrit and Kanarese and is said to have been learned in six languages. He is also said on many occasions to have defended the Jaina faith in public assemblies. In 1604 he completed an exhaustive grammar of the Kanarese language in 592 Sanskrit sūtras, accompanied with a gloss (vṛitti) and a commentary (vyākhyā) in the same language. The sūtras or mnemonic lines alone would fill but a few pages, but the full commentary accompanying them expands the book to 50 times that bulk. The work is entitled **Karnáṭaka Sabdánusásanam.** It is enriched with references to numerous previous authorities and quotations from leading Kanarese writers. The author earnestly vindicates the claim of Kanarese to receive as serious treatment as Sanskrit; and says that his aim has been to bring the language to the notice of the learned, to promote its cultivation, and to help to elegance and precision in its use. Although the work is in Sanskrit, it deserves a place in any history of Kanarese literature, because it is the most important grammar of the language, being fuller than the Śabdamaṇidarpaṇa or any other.[1]

The second writer was *Shaḍakshara Deva*, a Liṅgā-yat of Yelandur and head of a neighbouring *maṭha*. He is said to have shown poetic talent from the age of eleven. He composed poems both in Sanskrit and Kanarese. He wrote three works in Kanarese—*viz.* *Rājaśekhara Vilāsa* (1657), *Vṛishabhēndra Vijaya* (1671) and *Śabara Śaṅkara Vilāsa.* The second of these is the story of Basava retold in champu. The third describes one of the *līles* of Śiva. But it is his earliest work, the **Rájasekhara,** on which his fame chiefly rests. It divides with the *Jaimini Bhārata* the distinction of being the most highly esteemed poem in the language. It is written in champu of the best period. Although many metres are used, there is no shaṭpadi. The poem is an elaboration of the story told in the *Bhāva-chintā-ratna* (see p. 71). The following is an outline of the plot:

Rājaśēkhara, the hero of the story, is the son of Satyendra Choḷa, ruling at Dharmāvatī. He forms a very intimate friendship with Mitavachana, the son of the prime minister, who has been brought up with him. Together they conduct a victorious campaign against Ceylon, where Rājaśēkhara weds the king's daughter. Some time after his return to the capital, he receives a gift of two spirited horses from the Rāja of Sindh, and proposes to his friend that they should ride them through the crowded town. Mitavachana earnestly tries to dissuade him, reminding him that any loss of life caused is punishable by death, and that

[1] It has been published in Kanarese and Roman characters, and with English translation of the sūtras, by Mr. Lewis Rice in the *Bibliotheca Carnatica* (1890). A second edition is being prepared by Mr. Narasiṁhāchārya.

it is his father's boast that he will carry out the law impartially, however high the rank of the defaulter. Rājaśēkhara replies that he will take all the consequences upon himself. They set out, and Mitavachana, unable to control his horse, runs over and kills a boy. The bereaved mother appeals to the king. Rājaśēkhara admits that he alone is to blame, and is put to death. In grief thereat, Mitavachana kills himself; whereupon his father and mother also commit suicide. Rājaśēkhara's mother, the queen, and his widow are both in the very act of doing the same, when Śiva intervenes, raises to life all those who have died, commends Satyendra Choḷa for his unflinching consistency, and takes him to the joys of heaven.

The third writer, *Lakshmīśa*, a Śrī-Vaishṇava Brāhman of Dēvanūr in Kadur tālūk, is the author of the **Jaiminí Bhárata,** which is more famous than any other work of Kanarese literature, esteemed alike by learned and unlearned, and universally studied. Little is known of the poet, and his exact date is not yet determined. An initial date is given by the fact that he has imitated a number of verses from Virūpāksha (1585). As the earliest reference yet found to him is by Lakshma-kavi (1724), and thenceforth he is frequently mentioned, it is probable that he lived in or about the close of the seventeenth century. Unlike the Jaina poets, he does not name his predecessors. His poem is written throughout in shaṭpadi, and is the best specimen of that style. It is a free rendering of a Sanskrit work which bears the name of *Jaimini Bhārata* or *Aśva-Jaimini*, ascribed to the legendary sage Jaimini. The narrator of the story is Jaimini-muni, who tells it to Janamejaya. The subject is the wanderings of the horse appointed for Yudhishṭhira's horse-sacrifice. It, therefore, corresponds to a portion of the Aśvamedha Parva of the *Mahābhārata*; but it differs widely from the Sanskrit in details. The real motive of the poem is to extol Kṛishṇa. His greatness and the magical power of meditation on his name constitute the recurring theme throughout. The name of Kṛishṇa of Dēvāpura occurs in the closing stanza of each chapter. The following is an outline of the story :

A horse-sacrifice, it must be remembered, was in ancient times a proof of universal sovereignty. A horse had to be set free to roam for a year through neighbouring countries, and an army followed to overthrow any sovereign who dared to detain it. Yudhishṭhira, having overcome the Kauravas, determines to perform such a sacrifice. Bhīma is first sent to seize a horse from the neighbouring country of Bhadrāvatī, whose king he defeats. He then visits Kṛishṇa at Dwāraka and brings him to Hastināvatī. The horse is sent forth, bearing on its head a gold plate with a challenge to any king to detain it ; and is followed by Arjuna and an army and Kṛishṇa. It wanders in turn to Mahishmatī, Champakāpura, Strī Rājya (the Women's Realm, *i.e.* the Pāṇḍya and Malayālam countries), the Rākshasa country, Maṇipura (identified with a city in the south of the Mysore Province), Ratnapura, Sāraswata, and Kuntala, and finally crossing an arm of the sea (probably the Raṇ of Kach), returns, *via* Sindh to Hastināpura, the vanquished kings following in its train. The geography is partly imaginary.

The interest of the poem consists largely in its episodes, of which four may be mentioned : (1) In *Champakapura* the prince, Sudhanwa, is punished for delay in going to battle by being plunged into a caldron of boiling oil, but by meditation on Kṛishṇa he is able to remain in it, cool and uninjured. (2) At Maṇipura, the ruler is Babhru-vāhana, a natural son of Arjuna himself ; and Arjuna is under a curse to be slain by his hand. He is accordingly slain and his head cut off, but by means of the stone *sañjīvaka* and Kṛishṇa's blessing, he is restored to life. At this point the story is told at length of how Rāma fought with his sons, Kuśa and Lava. (3) At Mayūradhvaja's court in Ratnapura Kṛishṇa appears in the disguise of a mendicant Brāhman, who says that a lion has seized his son and refuses to release him, unless it is given instead one half of the king's body. The queen and heir-apparent both offer their lives as ransom, but are rejected. On the king's preparing to give his life, Kṛishṇa reveals himself. (4) At Kuntala the story is told of the romantic early career of the king Chandrahāsa, whose life was repeatedly plotted against by the previous king's minister, Dushṭabuddhi, but the minister's schemes all turned against himself, and as the result of them Chandrahāsa weds the minister's daughter and comes to the throne ; while the minister himself and his son and his hired assassins all meet with their death.

Extract from the *Jaimini Bhārata* by Lakshmīśa (XXX, 24-33). c. A.D. 1700

CHANDRAHĀSA AND VISHAYE

NOTE.—Dushṭabuddhi, prime minister of Kuntala, pays a visit to the tributary prince of Chandanāvatī. Before leaving he tells his daughter, Vishaye, that he will seek her a suitable husband ; and he leaves his son Madana as regent. Arrived at

Chandanāvatī, he recognizes in Chandrahāsa a prince of that place, the boy whom the Brāhman astrologers had previously indicated as destined to become ruler of Kuntala, and whom he thought he had killed in infancy, having paid hired assassins to murder him. So he now resolves to compass his death by poison. Pretending friendship, he sends him with a letter to his son, Madana. Chandrahāsa arrives in the outskirts of Kuntalapura, takes his meal in the royal garden, and falls asleep under a mango tree. Just then Vishaye has strayed from her companions to gather flowers ; and sees him asleep, and falls in love with him. From this point the poet proceeds as follows :

Listen, O king ! While thus the maiden gazed,
With heart enamoured, on that princely form,
So beauteous in its youthful grace, and now
So deep in slumber wrapt, her eyes discerned
A palm-leaf scroll tied in his garment's hem,
Which lay full loose outspread upon the ground.
By sudden impulse moved, she forward stepped, and quick
Drew forth the scroll. And then, with wonderment,
She found 'twas by her own dear father writ.
Elate with joy, she opened it, and read—

" His Excellency Dushṭabuddhi,
First Minister of Kuntala's fair realm,
To Madana, his much beloved son,
A father's blessing sends. No common man
Is he who brings this note. 'Tis plainly shown
That this same Chandrahāsa shall become
The sovereign lord of Kuntala. Bethink
What promise this holds forth for me and mine,
And how by us he should esteemed be.[1]
Wherefore make no delay ; nor idly ask
His birth or rank, his prowess or his fame.
But forthwith give him *vishava*, displayed
In such wise as to stir his heart's desire.
So shalt thou bring a royal benefit
To all our house. Farewell."

—Now *vishava*
Doth "poison" mean. And such the writer meant.
But where is he can alter by one jot

[1] In the original the ambiguity of the message depends on two possible ways of dividing *mahāhita* ("great friend" or "great enemy") and *sarvathāmitra* ("in all respects a friend" or "in all respects an enemy"), and on the two meanings of *mōhisu* ("desire" or "fall in love with"). As it is impossible to reproduce these in English, I have tried to imitate the ambiguity in another way.

What Destiny hath on the forehead writ?
And so it was. That gentle maiden pure,
Whose heart was full of tender hopes of love,
Remembering oft what, ere her father went,
He promised her,—that he a bridegroom fit
Would find and send—saw here the promise kept,
In such wise as should bring a royal benefit
To all their house. Since this most princely youth
Was marked by Fate to be the sovereign lord
On Kuntala's wide realm, what need to ask
His birth, his rank, or deeds already done.
"My father writes to give him *Vishaye*.
"'Tis well. But by some mere mischance my name
"Is wrongly writ. From this one letter's fault
"Lest mischief fall, I will amend it straight."

Upon the mango bark within her reach
A gum exuding trickled down. This served
For ink. And with the point of finger-nail
For pen, she deftly scratched the palm-leaf scroll,
And changed the *va* to *ye*. Then fastened swift
The seal as 'twas before, and tied the note
Once more within the garment's hem; and turned
To leave the place—yet treading soft, lest sound
Of rustling feet and bangles should betray
From whence she swiftly came. So she rejoined
Her folk.

But when they looked upon her face,
They noted there a new-born light, as of
Some happy secret found. They questioned her—
"How now?" they said, "where didst thou stray so long?
"And what doth please thee so?" But she was coy,
And would not tell. Whereat they laughing said—
"Thy face is like a book that can be read.
"As well might wand'ring zephyr try to keep
"The secret of the scented cinnamon grove
"As thou to hide thy heart's new happiness.
"Well, well! Secrets will out; and eftsoons we
"Thy secret too shall know."

She sweetly smiled,
And strove by forcèd merriment to hide
How fast her heart did leap;—till evening fell,
And to the town they bent returning steps.

It was the Marriage Season of the year.
The jocund sounds of wedding-songs and dance,
Of tabret, drum and tinkling cymbal, filled
The air; and troops of joyous matrons passed,

Busy with bridal rites. 'Twas such
Auspicious sounds and sights did greet the path
Of love-lorn Vishaye. The very gods
Did smile upon her hopes.

VAISHṆAVA LITERATURE AT THE COURT OF THE RĀJAS OF MYSORE

During the seventeenth and eighteenth centuries the patrons of Kanarese literature were chiefly the Rājas of Mysore, who had become independent from about 1610. At the same time they began to withdraw from the Liṅgāyat faith, and to adopt the worship of Vishṇu. They also commenced to extend their narrow territory, and to build up a strong kingdom by absorbing the surrounding pāḷeyagāris.

Histories. Several of the books of the Mysore period belong to the department of *History*. This had hitherto been represented mostly by inscriptions, many of which were elaborate compositions in verse and prose by distinguished scholars. Now it took more and more the form of books. Among these may be named *Kaṇṭhīrava Narasa Rāja Charitra*, by Nanjakavi; and *Kaṇṭhīrava Narasa Rāja Vijaya*, by Govinda Vaidya, both dealing with that rāja's reign (1638-59); *Deva Rāja Vijaya*, a metrical history of the reign of Doḍḍa Deva Rāja (1659-72), by Channārya; *Chikka Deva Rāja Yaśo-bhūshaṇa* and *Chikka Deva Rāja Vamsāvaḷi* (1672-1704), by Tirumalayengar; and *Maisūru Arasugaḷa Pūrvābhyudaya*, by Puṭṭaiya (1713). This last was one of the chief authorities used by Wilks in his *History of Mysore*. The manuscript was fortunately saved from among many which Tīpu Sultan had contemptously ordered, in 1796, to be taken for boiling the gram for the horses. In this connection mention may suitably be made of the *Rajēndra-nāme*, or Chronicles of the Coorg Rājas, by Vīra-rājendra, of Mercara (1808); of which there is an English translation by Lieutenant Abercrombie (Mangalore).

Chikka Deva Rāya's reign (1672-1704) calls for especial mention in connection with Kanarese literature. He had spent his early life in Yelandūr, and must have been in that town when the *Rājaśēkhara* was written. He formed there an intimate friendship with a Jaina scholar, named Vishālāksha Paṇḍit, who afterwards shared his captivity, when for 13 years (1659-72) he was kept in confinement in an obscure fort by his uncle, the reigning prince, and who ultimately became his first prime minister. His after ministers also were great scholars and authors; and doubtless these circumstances encouraged him in his patronage of literature. He caused a valuable library to be made of historical materials, including copies of the inscriptions in his dominions. Unfortunately, most of these were destroyed by Tīpu.

The rāja himself is credited with the authorship of several books. Two of these are prose commentaries—on the Sanskrit Bhāgavata, and on the later parvas (XII-XVIII) of the Mahābhārata. Another, the *Gīta Gopāla*, consists of songs in praise of Kṛishṇa, with prose summaries. But the best known is the *Chikka Deva Rāja Binnapam* (or "King's Petition"). This is a series of thirty verses on religious subjects, each followed by a prose amplification in the form of a prayer to Nārāyaṇa. The prose is in Old Kanarese, and professes to give the gist of Viśishṭādvaita doctrine for the benefit of all, in accordance with Bhagavad-gītā, ix, 32. All his works, however, make considerable mention of the author's territorial conquests.

The rāja was doubtless aided in the composition of his works by **Tirumalárya**, or Tirumalayengar, who had grown up with him, and been his companion in study. He was a great favourite with his sovereign, and became, first, court poet, and then, minister. Beside the two histories already mentioned, he wrote a work on rhetoric, entitled *Apratima-vīra-charitra* ("History of a Peerless Hero"), in which every illustrative stanza is in praise of his royal patron.

Chikupádhyáya, called also Lakshmīpati, another minister, was a very prolific author, and wrote some thirty works in champu, sāṅgatya and prose. He appears to have been a very zealous propagator of the

Vaishṇava faith. Several of his works are translations from the Sanskrit, including two versions of the *Vishṇu Purāṇa*, one in champu, the other in prose. Three are from the Tamil, *viz. Divya-sūri-charitre*, a history of the Twelve Āḷvārs; the *Artha-pañchaka*, or "Five Truths," of Pillai Lokāchārya, a principal Teṅgalai authority, who is said to have lived in the thirteenth century; and a commentary on the *Tiruvāyi-moḷe* of Nammāḷvār. Six are in praise of Raṅganātha of Seringapatam, the local form under which Vishṇu is worshipped. Several are *māhātmyas*, or commendations of Vaishṇava sacred places. They treat of Kāñchī, Mēlkōṭe, Tirupati, Śrīraṅgam, Seriṅgapatam, and Gopālswami Hill (near Guṇḍalpeṭ). Encouraged by him, many works of the same character were written by others.

Singarárya, another poet of Chikka Deva Rāja's court, and brother of Tirumalārya, has the distinction of having written what, until recent years, was the only drama in Kanarese literature. It is entitled *Mitravindā Govinda*. It is a free rendering of the Sanskrit *Ratnāvali* ("Pearl Necklace") attributed to king Harshadeva of Kanauj. In the original, it is a story of an amour between Udayana, king of Vatsa, and a maiden of the court, who is ultimately discovered to be the Princess Ratnāvali of Ceylon, who had been shipwrecked on the coast. It is a mark of the strong Vaishṇava enthusiasm of the time that, in the later work, Kṛishṇa is made the hero, instead of king Udayana. The heroine also is renamed Mitravindā; and the names of the other characters have been correspondingly altered.

Honnamma, a Śūdra woman, attendant on the queen, and called from her occupation "Sañchiya Honni," or "Honni of the betel bag," was a pupil of Singarārya's. She showed literary talent, and wrote in sāṅgatya a a book entitled *Hadibadeya-dharma* ("the Duty of a Faithful Wife"), in which she cites illustrations from the Epics and Manu.

The great literary activity of the Vaishṇavas in the seventeenth and early eighteenth centuries is further evidenced by the number of **fresh presentations of the Vaishnava classics** which appeared at this time.

The Bhārata is represented by the *Jaimini Bhārata*, by the *Lakshma-kavi Bhārata* (c. 1728), and by a translation of the *Bhagavad-gītā* by Nāgarasa of Paṇḍharpur, who gave a Kanarese rendering in shaṭpadi for each verse of the original.

Veṅkayārya, a Mādhva Brāhman, who was a Haridāsa of Penukoṇḍa region, reproduced the story of Kṛishṇa as contained in the tenth chapter of the Bhāgavata, in a work called *Kṛishṇalīlābhyudaya*.

Then there were no less than three fresh versions of the Rāmāyaṇa in whole or part. Tirumala-vaidya (c. 1650) completed the work of Kumāra Vālmīki by rendering into Kanarese the *Uttara-kāṇḍa*, the only portion of Vālmīki's Rāmāyaṇa which the earlier poets had left untranslated. Timmarasa (c. 1650) translated the abridged version of the story of Rāma, which forms an episode in the Forest Section of the Mahābhārata, where it is told by Mārkaṇḍeya to Yudhishthira. He entitled it *Mārkaṇḍeya Rāmāyaṇa*. Another rendering is the *Ānanda Rāmāyaṇa* by Timmārya, of Sādali near Anekal (c. 1708). Of him it is said that, although he was without scholarly education, a natural poetic gift showed itself in him from his fifteenth year ; and every morning he would pour forth his stanzas before his god, Timmarāya-swāmī, while a relative noted them down. This is probably typical of the way in which many Indian books have been written. The vaidika Brāhman in his *agrahāra* is a leisurely person; and before or after his ablutions, when the body was fresh, the intellect clear, and the devotional feelings stimulated by worship, he would sit in the open air in a retired spot, and compose and chant his stanzas, and embellish them with the pictures of sunrise, sunset or other seasonal changes, with which they abound.

The latter half of the eighteenth century was not favourable to authorship, as the country was frequently overrun by alien armies, and the throne of Mysore was occupied by the Muhammadan rulers—Haidar Ali and Tīpu Sultan.

JAINA WRITERS OF THE PERIOD

Although the Jainas had lost their former predominant position, their continued zeal for their religion is shown by the fact that in 1603 the colossal statue of Gommaṭeśvara at Yēnūr was sculptured. A re-anointing of the statue at Śravaṇa Beḷgoḷa in 1612 is described by the poet Pañchabāṇa of that town in his *Bhujabali-charitre* (1614). In 1646, the Kārkaḷa image also was re-dedicated. The history of this image and of Gommaṭa is given by Chandrama of the Tuluva country in his *Kārkaḷa-Gommaṭeśvara-charitre.*

Occasionally the Jainas were subject to persecution. The Telugu pāḷeyagār Jagaddeva-rāya of Channapatna even went so far as to suppress the worship of Gommaṭa. Not long after, however, his dominions were annexed by Mysore; and on appeal being made to the rāja, and the antiquity of the worship proved by the numerous śāsanas, the priests, who had retired to Gersoppa, were recalled, and the worship resumed. These facts are mentioned by Chidānanda-kavi (c. 1680) in his *Muni-vamśābhyudaya*, a genealogical account of the Jaina munis.

In addition to these works, and to Bhaṭṭākalaṅka's great grammar (1604) already mentioned, the following Jaina works belong to the seventeenth century:—*Bijjala-rāja-charitre*, which gives the Jaina version of Basava's life at the Kalyāṇa court; *Jina-muni-tanaya*, a cento on morals from the Jaina standpoint; and *Rāmachandra-charitre*, a new version of the Rāmāyaṇa story, commenced by Chandraśekhara (c. 1700) and completed by Padmanābha (1750).

Our account of the Jaina literature in Kanarese may be closed with the mention of the *Rājāvaḷi-kathe*, a prose summary of Jaina history and traditions, drawn up by Devachandra (1838) for a princess of the Mysore royal family. It has been of great assistance as a guide to the history of Jaina literature. The same scholar wrote a *Rāmakathāvatāra* (prose) based on the Pampa Rāmāyaṇa.

LIṄGĀYAT WRITERS OF THE PERIOD

In addition to the writings of Shaḍakshara-deva already mentioned, the following are the most noticeable Liṅgāyat writers of the period under review:

Basava-liṅga (1611) wrote *Śivādhikya-purāṇa*, on the pre-eminence of Śiva, and in it he incidentally justifies the reception of even the lowest classes into the Liṅgāyat community.

Siddha-nañjeśa, a guru of Nandial (c. 1650), wrote the history of the poet Rāghavāṅka; and also the *Guru-rāja-charitre*, or "History of the Great Gurus," which is a very useful account of the Vīraśaiva gurus, āchāryas, saints and poets. It contains also an account of Śiva's twenty-five *līles*.

Kavi-Mādaṇṇa (c. 1650) retold the story of Nannayya, a contemporary of Basava's, whose devotion is often referred to in Liṅgāyat literature, on account of his having cut off his own head to do honour to his guru.

Śānta-liṅga-deśika (1672), setting out to tell more fully in prose the stories briefly referred to in the *Bhairaveśvara-kāvya* of Kikkēri Nanjuṇḍa (c. 1550), enlarged his scope, and drawing tales from a wide circle of early writings, finally produced a collection of 81 tales and 618 *vākyas*. Apart from the tales, it is of considerable value owing to the fact that it gives incidentally much information about Vīraśaiva writers and their works. It is entitled *Bhairavesvara-kāvyada-Kathā-sūtra-ratnākara* ("Mine of Stories from the Bhairaveśvara-kāvya").

Liṅgāyatism received a severe blow when the Jaṅgama priests were massacred and the Liṅgāyat maṭhas destroyed by Chikka Deva Rāja, about 1680; and there appear to have been few Liṅgāyat writers for some time after. But Marulu-siddha (c. 1700), in his admiration for Basava, made an enumeration in prose of the miracles wrought by him, in thought, word or deed, and entitled it "The Marvels (*pavāḍa*) of Basava-rāja."

They had now grown to be no less than 360. The *Brahmottara-kāṇḍa*, a favourite Śaiva work, also probably belongs to this period.

WORKS ON ADVAITA PHILOSOPHY

We have thus far spoken of Kanarese works on three religions, but have said nothing of works on the Advaita philosophy. This has been because all works on this subject had hitherto been in Sanskrit. In the seventeenth century, this form of religion also was brought within reach of the Kanarese reader by Raṅganātha, called also Raṅgāvadhūta. As he appears to have been a disciple of the author of the *Bhakti-rasāyana* (c. 1650), his date is about 1675. At the opening of his work he thus justifies his use of the vernacular:

Scorn not my words because I seek
In common speech deep truths to speak.
A glass may lack a Sanskrit name,
Yet show one's features all the same.

The way to bliss is hard to find
When wrapped within a Sanskrit rind;
But, told in homely Kanarese,
Is free for every man to seize.

'Tis then like plantain's luscious pulp
When stripped of intervening skin;
Or cocoanut which, broken, shows
The rich sweet milk which lies within.

If one's intent to gain release
From bonds that bind the soul,
What matters if he reach that goal
By Sanskrit or by Kanarese?

The book is entitled **Anubhavámrita,** or "Nectar of Fruition." It is written in shaṭpadi, and expounds the expression *Tat twam asi* ("THAT art thou"), the doctrines of the Universal Soul (ātman) and of Illusion (māyā), the mode of attaining emancipation, and the worship of the Absolute (nirguṇārādhane), and other matters. The work is still studied as a leading text-book of the Vedānta in Kanarese. On it is largely based another well-known work, the *Jnāna-sindhu* ("Ocean of Knowledge"), by Chidānandāvadhūta (c. 1750). The epithet *avadhūta*, which both writers bear, signifies that they claimed to have cast off all family and property ties.

COLLECTIONS OF SHORT STORIES

Collections of short stories form another branch of literature which, popular at all times, flourished in this period. Most of these collections are in prose, and have a very large reading public. They are generally from Sanskrit originals, and in one form or another are known all over India. The famous *Bṛihat-kathā*, or "Great Story Book," of Guṇāḍhya was, as we have seen (pp. 28 and 38), rendered into Kanarese very early. Another such collection, based on the *Bhairaveśvara-kāvya*, has also been already mentioned (p. 94). Other very popular ones are the following:

The *Pañchatantra.* A champu version of this has already been mentioned as having been made by Durgāsiṁha as early as 1145. The same stories, however, are found besides in more than one prose version in Kanarese, the order of the tales varying somewhat in different recensions.

This famous work corresponds in a general way to the *Fables of Bidpay* or *Pilpay*, made known in Europe through a translation from the Arabic. Bidpay and Pilpay are indeed believed to be corruptions of the Sanskrit *vidyāpati*, "learned man." The work relates how some unpromising princes were taught political science by a clever minister under the guise of stories and fables about animals.

It receives its name from its "five chapters," which treat of as many conditions of political success. The first, *Mitrabheda*, "the Sowing of Dissension among allied enemies," is illustrated by the story of a lion and a bull, who were close friends until a jackal poisoned the mind of each against the other. The second, *Mitralābha*, or the "Acquisition of Allies," is illustrated by the tale of a tortoise, deer, crow and mouse, whose friendship proved useful to them all. Chapter iii, *Kākolūkīya*, or the "War between the Crows and the Owls," illustrates the danger of alliance between those whose conflicting interests make them natural enemies. Chapter iv, *Labda-pranāśa*, "The Loss of what has been Gained," enforces the warning that what has been acquired may again be lost, and that opportunities not utilised may never return. This is illustrated by several stories, the chief of which is about a monkey, which, having once escaped from the clutch of a crocodile, could not be caught a second time. Chapter v, *Aparīkshita-kārita*, "Precipitate Action," teaches that actions done without due consideration may lead to disaster, as, *e.g.* when the owner of a mungoose, through not waiting to investigate, slew the faithful creature which had saved the life of his child.

Battīsa-puttaḷi-kathe, a collection of thirty-two stories about Vikramāditya, supposed to be told to Bhoja Rāja by the thirty-two images which adorned the steps of his throne.

Bētāḷa-pañchaviṁśati-kathe, which exists in three forms, champu, tripadi and prose. It tells how Vikrama, of Ujjayini, in order to obtain certain magical powers, is directed to remove a corpse from a tree by night in perfect silence. On each of twenty-five attempts a *vētāḷa* (a goblin or sprite) accosts him and tells him some story involving a knotty problem. His interest being aroused, he is led to speak, and so to fail of his object.

Śuka-saptati, seventy tales, related by a parrot to a married woman whose husband was away on his travels.

Haṁsa-viṁśati-kathe, twenty tales by a swan.

Kathā-mañjari, and *Kathā-saṅgraha*, tales, often with morals, from various sources, which include the Epics and Purāṇas.

Tennāla-rāmakṛishṇana-kathe, a collection of laughable anecdotes of the court jester at Ānegundi, in the time of Kṛishṇa Rāya, of Vijayanagar (1508-30). The king and his chief minister appear in many of the stories. It may be well to mention that Tennāla Rāmakṛishṇa was not only a jester; he was a scholarly Brāhman who, under the name of Rāmaliṅga, wrote several works in Telugu.

A Specimen of Kanarese Humour

TENNĀLA RĀMAKṚISHṆA AND THE HUNCHBACKED MAN

When one day Tennāla Rāmakṛishṇa had played on the king a practical joke of more than usual audacity, the king was so angered that he determined that the jester should die. He ordered that he be buried in the earth up to his neck, and trampled to death by elephants. The bodyguard accordingly took Tennāla Rāmakṛishṇa to the open plain outside the city, dug a pit, placed him in it, and shovelled the earth around him, leaving his head exposed. They then went off to fetch the royal elephants. While they were gone, a hunchbacked man came that way ; and seeing a man's head projecting from the ground, asked in astonishment how he had managed to get buried like that. Tennāla Rāmakrishṇa replied that for years he had suffered much from having a hunchback, and had spent his all on doctors, but none of them had been able to cure him ; that some one had suggested that if he got buried up to his neck in the ground, his back would straighten of itself. Being very anxious for relief, he had got his friends to bury him. What he now wanted was that some one should kindly dig him out. The hunchbacked man at once set to work and released him. Then Tennāla Rāmakṛishṇa expressed great delight, and said, "See, I have lost my hunchback, and am perfectly straight again! Now *you* get in, and lose *your* hunchback." So the man got in, and Tennāla Rāmakṛishṇa filled in the earth : and then went his way and hid himself. When the bodyguard returned with the elephants, they were astonished to find buried in the ground a man other than the one they had put there. Having heard the man's story, they reported the matter to the king, who laughed so heartily at his jester's wit and ingenuity, that he forgot his anger, pardoned the offender and restored him to his office.

VIII

THE MODERN PERIOD

NINETEENTH CENTURY

With the nineteenth century begins an entirely new period of Kanarese literature, brought about by the influence of English rule in India, the impact of European civilisation, and the introduction of Western scientific methods of research and ideals of scholarship. The reorganisation of the education of the country on Western lines has largely increased the reading public, and extended the knowledge of and desire for literature, which now takes the form almost entirely of prose.

NEW CLASSES OF WORKS

The scope of this book, which treats rather of India's heritage from the past than of its productions in the present, as well as limitation of space, forbid any attempt to enumerate the authors and writers of this period. Their number has been very great, especially during the past fifty years. It will be sufficient to indicate the classes of works most characteristic of it, and to name a few examples.

i. Educational and informational works have been produced in large numbers and of steadily increasing value. These have included works on linguistics, history, biography, mathematics, agriculture, hygiene, medicine, law and other subjects. Thus has been brought about the beginning of a scientific literature—all earlier works of quasi-scientific character being hopelessly out of date. Although works on astrology and omens are still much in demand, they will gradually yield to the advancing wave of exact science.

ii. *Ṭīkās*, or verbal paraphrases, of the chief Brāhmanical poems of the past have been prepared in large numbers, to bring them within the understanding of students. This does not extend, however, to the old classical Jaina works, which are still very much neglected owing to their religious standpoint being out of favour.

iii. A class of books very largely in demand consist of stories from the Epics and Purāṇas, in a new literary form which sprang up in the eighteenth century, and is called *Yaksha Gāna.* It is a sort of dramatic composition suitable for recitation before rustic audiences by professional or amateur actors. The earliest example with which I am acquainted was by Madhva Dāsa of Uḍupi. Śāntayya, a Brāhman of Gersoppa, who became Principal Sadar Amīn at Mangalore, wrote a large number of works in this style.

Dramatic works of a higher order are now being produced—a department of literature in which only a single specimen (p. 91) has been found in earlier centuries. During the past thirty years, however, quite a considerable number have been published. The Epics, Purāṇas and Kāvya literature supply an inexhaustible fund of material. Such stories as those of Śakuntalā, Hariśchandra, Nala and Prahlāda are favourite subjects. The *Rājaśekhara* has been dramatised; and several of Shakespeare's plays have been adapted. Among the earlier productions of this class may be mentioned the *Śakuntala* by Basavappa Śāstrī, court poet of Chāmarājendra Woḍeyar (1868-94) and the *Tapatī Pariṇaya* by Veṅkaṭavaradāchārya of Sargūr. One of the most prolific dramatic authors has been Beḷḷavi Narahari Śāstrī. Another is Śāma Rau. But it is almost invidious to mention names.

iv. Novels are becoming increasingly popular. Most of those hitherto published have been reproductions from English or Bengali. Several of the plays of Shakespeare have been reproduced in this form, *e.g.* *Bhrānti Vilāsa* (Comedy of Errors); also such works as Sir Conan Doyle's detective stories of Sherlock Holmes.

The Bengali novels of Babu Baṅkim Chandra Chaṭṭopādhyāya and of Surendra Nāth have been reproduced, chiefly by Mr. B. Veṅkaṭāchārya, a retired munsiff. The most esteemed of these are the *Durgēśa-nandinī* and *Devīchandhu-rāṇī*.

v. Periodical literature, in the form of daily or weekly newspapers, and monthly magazines, are characteristic of this period. Some of these are prepared especially to meet the needs of female readers. Others are representative of Government departments (*i.e.* the *Economic Journal*), or of particular classes in the community (*i.e.* the *Vokkaligara Patrike*). The *Vṛittānta Patrike*, a weekly published at Mysore, has, I believe, the largest circulation of any newspaper.

vi. All the various sects continue freely to produce works illustrative of their creeds and praising the deities of their choice. Many Brāhmanical works, including a prose version of the *Bhāgavata* (entitled *Kṛishṇa Rāja Vāṇivilāsa*) were produced under the patronage of Kṛishṇa Rāja Woḍeyar III (1799-1868). Other works are of the *Bhakti-sāra* class, or are expositions of the Vedānta. Some are the utterances of the modern theistic movement, or are exhortations to morality. Special mention may be made of the *Nīti-mañjari*, by Mr. R. Narasiṁhāchārya, which reproduces in ancient Kanarese poetic form portions of some of the striking moral treatises existing in Tamil, including the *Kurraḷ*, of Tiruvalluvar; the *Mūdarai* and *Nalvale*, of Auvai; the *Nāladiyār*, etc.

Christianity has entered the field with versions of the Bible, Biblical Commentaries, books for the instruction of the Indian Christian community in the history and teachings of Christianity, translations of such Christian classics as Bunyan's *Pilgrim's Progress* (*Dēśāntriya Prayāṇa* or *Yātṛika Sañchāra*), Augustine's *Confessions*, etc., and lyrics for use in Christian worship.

It deserves to be added that Kanarese is indebted to the missionaries probably for the introduction of printing, and certainly for the improvement of its typography by the preparation of fresh founts of beautiful type for the printing of successive editions of the Bible. Missionaries have also led the way in the careful study of the language and literature. Witness the *English-Carnātaca*, and *Carnātaca-English* Dictionaries prepared by Rev. W. Reeve, of Bellary; the scholarly *Kannaḍa-English Dictionary* and historical *Kannaḍa Grammar*, by Rev. F. Kittel; the same scholar's editions of the *Chhandombuddhi* and *Śabdamaṇidarpaṇa*; and useful anthologies, grammars, etc., by Revs. Moegling, Weigle, Würth, and others.

As a specimen of recent productions we have only space to quote the following:—

Mysore Royal Anthem

Refrain: Great Gaurī, thou lotus-eyed goddess benign,
Pour forth on our Rāja thy blessings divine.

Thou Lady celestial, of loveliest grace,
Upholding all being—unbounded as space.

As Indra the demons—Agastya the sea—
Thou makest all powers of evil to flee.

All good that men seek is by thy hand outpoured,
The Consort co-equal of Śambhu, thy Lord.

O Chāmuṇḍī, dark-visaged lady divine.
Watch over Thy namesake of Chāmēndra's line.

For our gracious and good Mahārāja we pray.
Oh cherish him, guide him, and guard him alway.

NOTE.—The vocabulary of this anthem is almost entirely Sanskrit, though the forms are Kanarese. Chāmuṇḍī is another name of Gaurī. Her temple on Chāmuṇḍī Hill looks down upon Mysore City. Like Krishṇa, she is represented as of dark-blue countenance. *Chāma*, a modification of Sanskrit *śyāma*, means "dark-blue" or "black." The founder of the present dynasty, and father of the reigning Mahārāja, bore the name of Chāma Rājēndra.

PRESENT POSITION AND PROSPECTS OF KANARESE LITERATURE

It has already been mentioned in the Preface, that by the researches, especially of the German missionaries and of Mr. Lewis Rice and his coadjutor and successor in the Archæological Department of the Mysore Government, the wealth of Kanarese literature has been made known, the chronological position of the chief writers determined, and a large amount of information about them made accessible. An extensive collection of manuscript work has been assembled in the Oriental Library, established in Mysore. Some important works have been edited in the *Bibliotheca Carnātica* under the auspices of the Mysore Government, and others by private scholars, especially in two series, entitled *Kāvya-mañjari* and *Kāvya-kalānidhi*, and are thus available for general study. Jaina works (but mostly Sanskrit with Kanarese *ṭīkās* or verbal commentaries) are being edited by B. Padmarāja Paṇḍita, who also publishes a monthly journal, *Jaina-mata-prakāśikā*, on Jaina subjects. Some Liṅgāyat works have been edited by Kari Basappa Śāstrī of Mysore, and others at Poona.

In May, 1915, while the present little book has been under preparation, an Association has been formed at Bangalore, under the auspices of the Mysore Government, and named the "Kannaḍa Sāhitya Parishad," or "Kannaḍa Academy." This association includes representatives from all parts of the Kanarese country. It has as its object not only the study of past literature and the encouragement of present writers of merit, but the cultivation and improvement of the language—*e.g.* by the unification of dialects, the fixing of scientific terminology, and the formation of a common literary style. These are matters of much importance, as the language is undergoing rapid changes, and is exposed to dangers which need to be held in check. It is evident that the bulk of the literature will henceforth be in prose instead of in verse, and that a vocabulary and style intelligible to all readers of ordinary education will more and more take the place of archaic words and forms. It behoves writers to see that in giving expression to the thoughts of a new age they do no violence to the genius of the language. Three examples will illustrate the dangers of a time like the present.

1. During the brief period of Muhammadan rule in Mysore, Persian was made the language of the courts, and large numbers of Persian words and idioms were needlessly imported into Kanarese. Many of these still survive in Government notifications and legal documents, and form an object lesson of how Kanarese ought *not* to be written. Again, at the present time, in the conversation of English-educated Kanarese persons, English expressions are being similarly imported wholesale, without any attempt at naturalisation. These reappear in hurriedly written newspaper articles, and, being widely read, are apt to affect the style of public speech, and denationalise and deprave the language.

2. One of the beauties of Kanarese is that all the pauses and intonations, which in English are represented by punctuation, are expressed by the vernacular idiom itself; so that no well-constructed Kanarese sentence requires any marks of punctuation whatsoever. Nevertheless, most modern Kanarese books are disfigured with all the cumbrous apparatus of Western commas, semicolons, inverted commas and marks of interrogation and exclamation. The result is, that there is growing up a slovenly mode of writing, in which the sense is no longer clear without these alien aids.

3. Another evil tendency appears in books rendered from Western languages by incompetent translators. Complicated sentences are reproduced in facsimile, in which one adverbial clause is subordinate to another, and that to a third. Such a mode of expression is wholly foreign to Kanarese idiom and destructive to good writing—a native Kanarese sentence, however lengthy, being always simple in structure and pellucid in meaning.

It is to be hoped that no encouragement will be given to the introduction of foreign idioms involving intricacy and obscurity; but that Western languages will be utilised only to *enrich* Kanarese literature (1) by fertilising it with new and noble thoughts, and (2) by lending it such additional vocabulary as is absolutely necessary to express the ideas that result from world-wide intercourse.

IX

SOME CHARACTERISTICS OF KANARESE LITERATURE

It will be helpful to the English reader if we mention a few characteristics of Kanarese literature, some of which will be found to be characteristic of other Indian languages as well.

1. It will be noticed that the interest of Kanarese writers is almost entirely *religious*. If we exclude grammatical and linguistic works, there is, until the nineteenth century, extremely little that is not connected with religion. The history is mostly sacred history or hagiology; the works of imagination centre round purāṇic and mythological subjects; and every book opens with a lengthy invocation of all the gods and saints of the author's sect. Secular history, except as represented by the records contained in *śāsanas* on stone or copper, begins to appear only at a late period.

2. The great bulk of the literature until the nineteenth century had been in *verse*. The Jaina poets used a form of composition called champu, in which passages of prose were interspersed among the metrical stanzas; but complete prose works have been comparatively few until recent years, when they have become common enough. To read Kanarese books in the ordinary tone of speaking is to miss much of their beauty; they are intended to be chanted. When thus chanted with correct phrasing and musical intonation, all the author's grace of alliteration, metaphor and metre are brought out, and the effect is highly pleasing. Even those who cannot follow the meaning will listen to such chanting with delight.

3. Literary and poetic usage demands the use of *archaic* forms and words, as well as of Sanskrit terms for common things. Hence the ordinary Kanarese man is no more able to follow the meaning of the great poets than an ordinary Englishman is to understand an Anglo-Saxon book. The books are written for scholars, not for the man in the street. In indigenous schools it is a common practice for boys to repeat large portions of such books as the *Jaimini Bhārata* without understanding in the least what it is all about.

4. Indians have great admiration for the wit and ingenuity shown in what is called *Ślēsha* or *double entendre*; and a writer's fame is much enhanced if his work abounds with stanzas which are capable of two or more meanings. This effect is facilitated by the fact that consecutive words are ordinarily run together, so that the letters are capable of being divided up in different ways. *The Pāṇḍava-Rāghavīya*, a Sanskrit work of the sixteenth century, is written throughout on this principle, so that, divided up in one way, it tells the story of the *Rāmāyaṇa* and divided up in another way, the story of the *Mahābhārata*! In English literature the practice of punning is confined to works which are semi-comic, such as some of the writings of Tom Hood.

From the use of *Ślēsha* and of archaic words and forms two results follow. The first is that the writings of the poets need to be elucidated by commentaries or *ṭīkās*, which give modern forms for ancient, and vernacular terms for Sanskrit, and which expound the double or treble meanings and the allusions to mythologic story. The other is that a Kanarese poem defies anything like literal translation into another language. To give any idea of the spirit of the original it would be necessary to paraphrase freely, to expand the terse and frequent metaphors into similes, and to give a double rendering of many stanzas. An example will make this clear. The opening stanza of the *Jaimini Bhārata* is given in Sanderson's translation as follows:

> May the moon-face of Vishṇu, of Devapura, always suffused with moonlight smile, full of delightful favour-ambrosial rays—at

which the chakora-eye of Lakshmī is enraptured, the lotus-bud heart of the devout expands, and the sea of the world's pure happiness rises and overflows its bounds—give us joy.

The following is an attempt, by means of a freer rendering, to retain something of the spirit of the original:

When the full moon through heaven rides,
Broad Ocean swells with all its tides;
The lotus blossom on the stream
Opens to drink the silv'ry beam;
And far aloft with trancèd gaze
The chakor bird feeds on the rays.

So, when great Vishṇu's face is seen,—
Whom men adore at Devapore—
Like to the sea, the devotee
Thrills with a tide of joy;
Like to the flower, that blissful hour
The heart of the devout expands;
And Lakshmī Queen, with rapture keen,
Watches with ever-radiant face
For her great Consort's heavenly grace.
O may that grace be ours!

5. There is a number of stock metaphors, drawn from the lotus, the carpenter bee, the tide, etc., of which Indian writers seem never to weary, and of which use is made with infinite ingenuity in practically every Indian poem. Some of these do not correspond with the facts of natural history, but are mere poetic conventions; such as that the chakora bird feeds only on the rays of the moon, that the lotus grows in rivers, that the Asoka tree has no fruit, and that the lily blooms only by night.[1] There is an interesting chapter on this subject in the *Kāvyāvalokana* of the twelfth century.

6. One misses in India the poetry of pure human love, which forms so large and rich an element in the

[1] Compare the popular, but erroneous, belief, current in Europe, that the ostrich hides its head in the sand to escape danger—an idea probably derived from some fable. Also the old Greek and Roman idea that the swan sings sweetly, especially when death approaches.

literature of the West. This is partly due to the very inferior position accorded to woman; but it is also largely due to the fact that marriages are arranged and consummated in very early life, so that neither men nor women ordinarily pass through that beautiful and romantic period of courtship, with all its mutual reverence, shyness and mystery, which is natural to full-grown unwedded youth. The practice of early marriage, it is true, safeguards youth from many serious dangers. But its unfortunate effect on literature is that the sweetheart is replaced by the courtesan; and instead of the healthy sentiment of a pure love we have nauseous passages of erotic description, which disfigure a very large proportion of the poetical writings. Against this may perhaps be set touching examples of wifely fidelity, such as Sītā, Damayantī and Sāvitrī.

7. I am afraid it must be confessed that Kanarese writers, highly skilful though they are in the manipulation of their language, and very pleasing to listen to in the original, have as yet contributed extremely little to the stock of the world's knowledge and inspiration. They excel in the grammatical study of their own language, and in description of the recurring phenomena of the seasons; but there is little original and imperishable thought on the questions of perennial interest to man. There are earnest calls to detachment from the world; but this, after all, is only a negative virtue. High counsels of morality are given; but they are too abstract; they lack embodiment in genuine historical characters. The legendary illustrations offered are marred by unreality, if not also by moral imperfection and faulty ideals. The writers are dominated by the depressing conception of life as either an endless and unprogressive round of transmigration or a quest of the tranquil dreamless sleep of nirvāṇa. Hence a lack of that which stimulates hope and inspires to great enterprises. Moreover, their thought moves ever within the circle of Hindu mythological ideas, and is not likely long to survive the passing of those ideas, which are now rapidly on the wane. Among their writers one looks in vain for any rousing

moral preacher comparable to the prophets of Israel, to the great Greeks and Romans, or such modern writers as Ruskin, Tolstoi and Carlyle. As historic testimony to a phase of human thought the literature is valuable. But while there is abundant evidence of earnest spirits perplexed with the mystery of the universe and seeking to know THAT which lies at the back of what is seen and temporary, there is no such answer to these questions of the heart as to provide permanent solace and inspiration. But a new and vitalising force has now entered the land. The people are learning the new truth that they are children of a Heavenly Father, that life is an education for something better, that self-sacrificing service of the brotherhood of mankind is nobler than a selfish asceticism, and that righteousness and sympathy are the qualities that unite to God—the true path of *yoga*. And so, conscience is awaking as never before, new ideals of integrity and duty are beginning to inspire the mind of the people, and before them shines a star of immortal hope.

X

KANARESE GRAMMARIANS

FROM a very early period Kanarese writers have shown marked eminence in the department of Grammar and allied subjects, such as Rhetoric and the Art of Poetry; and this subject demands a chapter to itself. It will be convenient to give a connected account of the works of the chief grammarians, although their works extend over several centuries. Most of these scholars belonged to the Jaina community, to which Kanarese literature owes so great a debt.

As early as. A.D. 600 Dēvanandi Pūjyapāda (see p. 27), wrote a Sanskrit grammar known as *Jainendra*, which is quoted by Vōpadeva (thirteenth century) as one of the eight original authorities on Sanskrit grammar. It is said to have received its name from the title, Jinendra, which Pūjyapāda bore. It has also the name of *Aneka-śēsha Vyākaraṇa* (See *Ind. Ant.* X, 75).

About 850 was published the *Kavirājamārga*, a work on ornate composition and rhetoric, fully illustrated by examples, and evidencing a popular interest in the subject, and a high state of development in its study (see page 25). It is to a large extent dependent on the *Kāvyādarśa*, "Mirror of Poesy," of Daṇḍin (sixth century).

About 990 Nāgavarma I wrote the *Chhandombudhi*, or "Ocean of Prosody," which, with additions by later scholars, is still the standard book on the subject of Kanarese prosody. It is based on the similar Sanskrit work by Piṅgaḷa. In the account of the *vṛitta* metres, each verse is so composed as to be an example of the metre described in it. It has been edited by Dr. Kittel

(Mangalore, 1875), who has added illustrations from various poets. Kittel's edition includes an account of shaṭpadi and other metres which were not invented till after Nāgavarma's time, but a description of which had been added in later manuscripts.

In the twelfth century (c. 1145), another grammarian of the same name, and hence known as *Nāgavarma II*, wrote two notable grammars of the language, one in Kanarese verse, the other in Sanskrit sūtras, which are the earliest known systematic treatises on the subject. The first is called *Śabda Smṛiti*, and forms the first part of a larger work, entitled *Kāvyāvalokana*, or "Treatise on the Art of Poetry." This is the fullest work in the language on the subject of poetical composition. Successive chapters treat of the Grammar of the language, Faults and Elegances in composition, Style, and Poetic Conventions. It is copiously illustrated with quotations from earlier writers, as well as with original stanzas. He followed it by a Sanskrit work, the *Karṇāṭaka-bhāshā-bhūshaṇa*, in which the grammatical rules are reduced to 269 *sūtras*, or mnemonic formulæ, each sūtra being accompanied by a *vṛitti*, or explanatory gloss, also in Sanskrit. The edition by Mr. R. Narasiṁhāchārya in the *Bibliotheca Carnātica* includes a Kanarese commentary probably belonging to the seventeenth century. Nāgavarma II also compiled a Sanskrit-Kanarese glossary, entitled *Vastu Kōśa*, which is the earliest work of its kind in Kanarese. It is composed in a variety of metres. Among other authorities, it quotes the *Amara Kōśa*.

In the next century (c. 1260) Kēśirāja wrote the *Śabdamaṇidarpaṇa*, or "Jewel-mirror of Grammar," which remains till now the standard early authority on the Kanarese language. The rules are written in *kanda* metre, and are accompanied by a prose *vṛitti*, or illustrative commentary, provided by the author himself. It was edited by Dr. Kittel (Mangalore, 1872), along with a commentary of probably the seventeenth century. Of this grammar Dr. Burnell says (*Aindra School of Grammarians*, pp. 8, 55): "The great and real merit of the *Śabdamaṇidarpaṇa* is that it bases its rules on independent research and the usage of writers of repute. In this way it is far ahead of the Tamil and Telugu treatises, which are much occupied with vain scholastic disputation." As Mr. Lewis Rice justly says: "This encomium is equally applicable to other Kanarese grammars, which had not been made public in 1875, when Burnell wrote. Nothing is more striking than the wealth of quotation and illustration from previous authors which these grammatical writings contain, and this gives them a high scientific as well as historical value."

In 1604 was published Bhaṭṭākalaṅka Deva's *Karṇāṭaka Śabdānuśāsana*, a fuller and more exhaustive grammar in 592 Sanskrit sūtras, accompanied with a gloss and commentary in the same language. See further, p. 83. Like his predecessors, he quotes numerous previous authors and Kanarese writers.

Other works useful to the student of the language, and illustrating the continuous interest in this subject, may be tabulated in chronological order. The letter J after a name denotes that the writer was a Jaina, and L a Liṅgāyat.

c. 1150. *Udayādityālaṅkāram*, by Udayāditya, a Choḷa prince, 72 stanzas on the art of poetry, largely based on Daṇḍin's *Kāvyādarśa*.

c. 1235. *Kabbigara-kāva*, by Āṇḍayya (J), a work written entirely without tatsamas. See p. 44.

c. 1300. *Amara-kōśa-vyākhyāna*, a valuable Kanarese commentary on the *Amara-kōśa*, by Nāchirāja (J).

c. 1350. *Karṇāṭaka-śabda-sāra*, a prose dictionary of 1,416 words.

1398. *Abhinava-nighaṇṭu*, or "New Lexicon," by Abhinava Maṅgarāja, based on the *Vastu-kōśa* of Nāgavarma II. It gives the Kanarese meanings of Sanskrit words.

c. 1450. *Chaturāsya-nighaṇṭu*, by Bommarasa (L); synonyms in 130 stanzas.

c. 1500. *Mādhavālaṅkāra*, a translation of Daṇḍin's *Kāvyādarśa*, by Mādhava, a chief of Hiriyur in Kuntala.

,, *Kavi-jihvā-bandhana*, by Īsvara Kavi; on prosody, rhetoric and other subjects.

c. 1530. *Kabbigara-kaipiḍi*, or "Poets' Vade-mecum," by Liṅga (L); a dictionary of synonyms in 99 verses, intended to aid the understanding of the

Śaiva poets. He was minister to the Rāya of Nuggehaḷḷi.

1533. *Kāvya-sāra*, a valuable anthology, by Abhinava Vādi Vidyānanda (J).

c. 1550. *Rasa-ratnākara*, by Sāḷva (J); a complete treatise on dramatic composition.

c. 1560. *Karṇāṭaka-śabda-mañjari*, a vocabulary of tadbhava and Kanarese words; by Toṭadārya (L).

c. 1600. *Karṇaṭāka-sanjīvana* (J), a glossary of words spelt with ṟa and ḷa.

,, *Nānārtha-ratnākara*, a glossary of Sanskrit words having several meanings, by Devottama (J).

,, *Navarasālaṅkāra*, by Timma; on rasa and rhetoric ornaments.

c. 1640. *Kavi-kaṇṭha-hāra*, "Poet's Necklace," a metrical repertory of synonym's, by Sūrya.

1700. *Apratima-vīra-charitra*, by Tirumalayengar, minister of Chikkadeva Rāya.

It is needless to refer to the many good modern grammars prepared for use in schools.

XI

SANSKRIT WRITERS IN THE KANARESE COUNTRY

An account of English Literature would scarcely be complete without some mention of Newton's *Principia* and Bacon's *Novum Organum*, although these were written in Latin. In like manner, many notable works have been written in the Kanarese country by Kanarese men, but in the Sanskrit language. It has already been stated that some of the early Jaina poets wrote in Sanskrit, *e.g.* Samantabhadra and Pūjyapāda Devanandi. Reference has also been made to various poets, such as Ponna (c. 950), Nāgavarma II (1120), Pālkurike Soma (c. 1195), and Shaḍakshara Deva (1657), who were equally facile in Sanskrit and Kanarese, and some of whom bore the honorific title, *ubhaya-kavi*, "Poets, both in Sanskrit and the vernacular." Mention has also been made of Bhaṭṭākalaṅka's Kanarese Grammar, written in Sanskrit (1604). A long list could doubtless be given of Sanskrit writers within the Kanarese area. The following are only a few of the more famous:

In the ninth century *Śaṅkarāchārya*, the great Advaitī philosopher, established his principal monastery at Śriṅgēri, where some think he died. Some of his commentaries may have been written there.

In 1085 *Bilhana*, a Kashmīrī Brāhman, who had settled at Kalyāṇa, wrote the *Vikramārkadeva-charitra*, a Sanskrit poem recounting the adventures and prowess of his patron, the Chālukya king, Vikrama (1076-1127). At the same court lived *Vijñāneśvara*, who there compiled the *Mitākshara*, which remains to this day a standard work on Hindu Jurisprudence. It concludes with the words: "On the face of the earth there has not been, there is not, and there never will be, a city like Kalyāṇa; never was a monarch seen or heard of equal to the prosperous Vikramārka."

In the thirteenth century *Madhvāchārya*, called also Ānandatīrtha (1199-1278), founded the Dvaita school of the Vedānta. He lived and established his principal *maṭha* at Uḍupi in the Kanarese country, where he wrote his commentaries. He exerted a powerful influence on Kanarese literature.

Early in the fourteenth century, *Vidyātīrtha*, guru of the Śriṅgēri maṭha, was a great exponent of Śaṅkara's philosophy; and *Jayatīrtha*, guru of the Uḍupi maṭha, of Madhvāchārya's.

Mādhavāchārya, called also Vidyāraṇya, wrote the *Sarva-darśana-saṅgraha*, or "Compendium of all the Philosophical Systems," and many other works. He was purohita and first minister of Bukka Rāya of Vijayanagar (1353-77). He succeeded Vidyātīrtha as guru of the Śriṅgēri maṭha. His own town was Hampe, where he died and where his tomb is still shown.

His brother *Sāyaṇa*, who died 1387, was the most celebrated commentator on the Vedas.

I believe that many of the gurus of the Śriṅgēri, Mēlkōṭe and Uḍupi maṭhas have been the authors of learned Sanskrit works.

LEADING DATES

Exact dates are in thick type. Other dates are approximately correct; but, if followed by a question mark, are more or less conjectural.

Rāshṭrakūṭas ruling at Mānyakheṭa in N. Karṇāṭaka, 820-973.
850 *Kavirājamārga.*
941 Adi Pampa's *Bhārata* and *Ādi Purāṇa.*
950 Ponna's *Śānti-purāṇa.*
Later Gaṅgas ruling at Talkāḍ in S. Karṇāṭaka, 900-1000.
978 *Chāvuṇḍa-rāya Purāṇa.*
990 Nāgavarma I's *Chhandombuddhi.*
1000-1050 Cholas overrun S. Karṇāṭaka.
Western Chālukyas ruling at Kalyāṇa in N. Karṇāṭaka, 973-1156.
993 Ranna's *Ajita-purāṇa*, etc.
1085 Bilhana and Vijñaneśvara.
1145 Durgāsiṁha's *Pañchatantra.*
Kalachuris ruling at Kalyāṇa in N. Karṇāṭaka, 1156-1186.
1160 Liṅgāyat Revival under Basava and Channabasava.
Hoysalas or Ballāl Rājas ruling at Dōrasamudra in S. Karṇāṭaka, 1040-1326.
1105 Nāgachandra's *Pampa Rāmāyaṇa.*
,, Kanti (poetess) and Rājāditya (mathematician).
1098 Rāmānujāchārya converts Hoysala Crown Prince to Vaishṇavism.
1112 Nayasena's *Dharmāmṛita.*
1145 Nāgavarma II's *Kāvyāvalokanam* and *Bhāshā-bhūshaṇa.*
1165 Harīśvara's *Girijā-Kalyāṇa.*
,, Rāghavāṇka, earliest writer of Shaṭpadi.
1170 Nemichandra's *Līlāvatī.*
1180 Rudrabhaṭṭa's *Jagannātha-vijaya.*
1195 Pālkurike Soma.
xii. cent. Transition from Ancient to Mediæval Kanarese.
1200 Devakavi's *Kusumāvali.*
1209, **1230** Janna's *Yaśodhara-charitre* and *Anantanātha-purāṇa.*
1232 Sāṅgatya first used by Siśumāyaṇa.
1235 Āṇḍayya's *Kabbigara-Kāva.*
1245 Mallikārjuna's *Sūkti-sudhārṇava.*
1260 Kesirāja's *Śabdamaṇi-darpaṇa.*
1275 *Kumudendu Rāmāyaṇa.*
1280 Madhvāchārya preaches Dvaita doctrine.
,, The temples at Haḷebīd and Java building.

1310-1326 Muhammadan invasions overthrow South India kingdoms.

The Vijayanagar Kingdom, 1336-1610.

1350-1387 Mādhavāchārya and Sāyaṇa flourish.

1369 Bhīma-kavi's *Basava-purāṇa.*

1385 Madhura's *Dharmanātha-purāṇa.*

,, Padmanāṅka's *Padmarāja-purāṇa.*

1419-46 Prauḍha Deva Rāya's reign.

Chāmarasa's *Prabhuliṅga-līle.*

Kumāra-Vyāsa's *Gadugina Bhārata.*

1470 Tōṇṭada Siddheśvara.

1500 Kumāra-Vālmīki's *Torave Rāmāyaṇa.*

,, Siṅgi-rāja's *Mala-basava-rāja-charitre.*

1500(?) Nijaguṇa-yogi's *Viveka-chintāmaṇi.*

1509-30 Kṛishṇa-deva-rāya's reign.

1510 *Kṛishṇa-rāya Bhārata.*

1513 Mallanārya's *Bhāva-chintā-ratna.*

1530 *Kannaḍa Bhāgavata.*

,, Kabbigara-kaipiḍi.

1533 Abhinava Vādi Vidyānanda's *Kāvya-sāra.*

1550 *Sāḷva-Bhārata.*

,, Purandara-dāsa and Kanaka-dāsa.

1557 Ratnākara-varṇi's *Aṇṇagaḷa-pada.*

1585 *Channabasava-purāṇa.*

xvi. cent. Transition from Mediæval to Modern Kanarese.

1600(?) Sarvajña-mūrti.

1604 Bhaṭṭākalaṅka's *Karṇāṭaka Śabdānuśāsana.*

Mysore Rajas become independent, and adopt Vaishṇavism, 1610.

1614 Pañchabāṇa's *Bhujabali-charitre.*

1646 *Kārkaḷa-Gommaṭeśvara-charitre.*

1650 *Bijjala-rāya-charitre.*

,, Siddha-nañjeśa's *Guru-rāja-charitre.*

1657 Shaḍakshara-deva's *Rājaśekhara Vilāsa.*

1672 Śāntaliṅga-deśika's *Stories from Bhairaveśvara-kāvya.*

1672-1704 Chikka Deva Rāya's reign.

Chikupādhyāya and Tirumalayeṅgār.

1675 *Anubhavāmṛita.*

1680 *Mitravindā-Govinda.*

,, Massacre of Jaṅgamas.

xvii. cent. The letter ṟa falls out of use.

1700 Lakshmīśa's *Jaimini Bhārata.*

,, Chandraśekhara's *Rāmachandra-charitre.*

1708 *Ānanda Rāmāyaṇa*

1728 *Lakshma-kavi Bhārata.*

,, *Kṛishṇa-līlābhyudaya.*

1761-99 Haidar Ali and Tīpu Sultan.

1838 Devachandra's *Rājāvaḷi-kathe.*

INDEX